P9-AFZ-023

G4
V37
2007
c.3

SHARE THE LIGHT

WITH THE GIFT OF A

B ♥ Ø ♥ Ø ♥ K

This material has been generously
provided by the Kwantlen University
College Buy-a-Book Campaign.

JAN 1 5 2008

BEING GENEROUS

Lucinda Vardey & John Dalla Costa

BEING GENEROUS

The Art of Right Living

ALFRED A. KNOPF CANADA

PUBLISHED BY ALFRED A. KNOPF CANADA

Copyright © 2007 Lucinda Vardey and John Dalla Costa

All rights reserved under International and Pan-American Copyright
Conventions. No part of this book may be reproduced in any form or by
any electronic or mechanical means, including information storage and
retrieval systems, without permission in writing from the publisher,
except by a reviewer, who may quote brief passages in a review.
Published in 2007 by Alfred A. Knopf Canada, a division of Random
House of Canada Limited. Distributed by Random House of Canada
Limited, Toronto.

Knopf Canada and colophon are trademarks.

www.randomhouse.ca

Library and Archives Canada Cataloguing in Publication
Vardey, Lucinda
Being generous : the art of right living / Lucinda Vardey and John
Dalla Costa.

ISBN 978-0-676-97883-4

1. Generosity. I. Dalla Costa, John II. Title.

BJ1533.G4V37 2007   177'.7   C2007-902460-2

First Edition

Printed and bound in the United States of America

2 4 6 8 10 9 7 5 3 1

For Edwina,
whose generosity is constant,
and
for Lewis,
whose creativity fills us still.

CONTENTS

O may I join the choir invisible
Of those immortal dead who live again
In minds made better by their presence: live
In pulses stirred to generosity,
In deeds of daring rectitude, in scorn
For miserable aims that end with self,
In thoughts sublime that pierce the night like stars,
And with their mild persistence urge man's search
To vaster issues.

So to live is Heaven:
To make undying music in the world, . . .

GEORGE ELIOT
Excerpt from "O May I Join the Choir Invisible"

Invitation

―――

"MAY I speak to you?" asked the man politely. I was the conspicuous Westerner in a mid-sized city in Japan, far off the usual tourist track. He wanted to practise his English. I said yes, of course, bowing slightly to him. Without being overt about it, my middle-aged interlocutor eventually got around to wondering why I was there—in that park, in that city, on a Sunday. His English was not developed enough for me to explain that I was going through what my bemused friends called a mid-life crisis, but what I considered a journey of self-discovery. I was without work and without plans, having left my job to look for something true, or more truly me. Visiting Japan was therefore both a break and a breaking free. I did not talk to the man about my faith as a Catholic, nor did I presume to explain this trip as existential restlessness. Yet through our fairly monosyllabic exchange, he came to sense my situation. Before leaving me to allow us to continue going our separate ways, this Japanese gentleman unrolled his Buddhist prayer beads from his wrist, and offered them to me. Touched by this gesture, I knew enough about the culture, with its risks of losing face, to accept. And before I could react or figure out how to reciprocate, he had gone.

On the bus back to my hotel, I held this gift in my hand and pondered the meaning of what had happened. His was an act of gracious courtesy and hospitality, an outreach of welcome to a stranger. Such simple, unexpected kindness had bridged a huge cultural divide, connecting us, despite depths of unfamiliarity, in the sunshine on a warm summer's day. Having grown up in a household with rosary beads, I knew that what I had received was also special on another level. Devotion beads are imbued with historical and theological symbolism, giving them a transcendent value. Yet they are also highly personal, almost intimate instruments of piety, which accrue a considerable patina of joy, sorrow and faith in repeatedly passing through one's fingers over days, months and frequently years of prayer. I was moved because I was seen, not merely recognized. By receiving these beads I felt a bit less lost, while still being out of place. And I carried away not only a reminder of that moment, but also a part of the giver. Most Westerners call these "worry beads." I eventually came to appreciate them as "why worry?" beads. And one year before I met my wife, and thirteen years before we began this book, I placed these beads on my prayer altar at home as a reminder of small generosities that can have unfathomable consequences.

Being generous, we have learned in our work as writers and as a married couple, is elemental to humanity. Across diverse cultures and beliefs, and despite many differences throughout history, the practice of generosity is universally revered as one of the highest qualities of the human heart. The good Samaritan is an archetypical model most people recognize, not only for going out of his way to take care of someone in need, but also for revealing, through kindness, what is familiar and deeply human about those who are otherwise regarded as strangers. As well as a mark of personal character, generosity is also an attribute of what people mean by civil society or civilization. Some of the most prestigious institutions of community—public schools, libraries, hospitals and universities—were founded and moulded in the restive generosity of committed volunteers or sponsoring philanthropists. Although generosity may well involve being charitable, not all charity qualifies as such. That is because, beyond the impulse of pity or sympathy, generous actions almost always undo disadvantage or hardship and contribute healing, thereby making possible a more humane future. An investment in positive change, the practice of generosity usually provides a spark of hope by which people themselves are transformed, enabled and revivified.

This book examines the joyful riches of generosity we, as its authors, have discovered to be personally fulfilling. Writing together (co-authoring as a married couple) has been a sort of litmus test for both the premise and the joys of what we call the art of right living, one we have embraced and held central in our lives. Each of us, in our own way, learned about being generous by osmosis. Our parents, while from quite contrasting cultures and in markedly different circumstances, exemplified daily attitudes and actions that, in hindsight, we have recognized as intrinsically generous. In southern England, one father and mother managed to balance making a living as artists while giving considerable time to the needs and creativity of their five children. No matter what the external or professional pressures, the priority at home was for expressions of kindness—inviting discussion, relishing the sharing of ideas and supporting inspiration. Small requests were accorded respectful attention: the mending of broken toys, wristwatches and torn clothes; helping with homework; and being the patient audience for endless music recitals and comedy skits. In small-town Canada, another father and mother confronted the hardships of settling in a foreign land while offering shelter, home-cooked meals and even sock darning to other new immigrants. Labouring long hours to make a living, they still made time within this exhausting cycle of work to ensure that the children would find opportunities that they, as parents, had never had. Humble luxuries, like television and telephone, were readily shared with neighbours who were without.

So we two grew up in households in which generosity was not an exceptional attribute but an ordinary, everyday constant. It was part of the equation for learning life's lessons, for dealing with conflicts and misunderstandings, and for nurturing creative gifts in ourselves as well as others. And it overflowed as an invisible assumption, permeating the interactions between family members while also conditioning the way we reached out to the world and others in the community. This default spirit of generosity was certainly shaped by similar religious backgrounds. With Italian and Irish Catholic roots, we grew up with the stories and doctrines that affirmed self-sacrifice in the service of others, or for a good and right cause. Like almost all of the world's major religions, Catholicism preaches charity, compassion and responsibility for community. However, being Catholic did not make us more generous. Our cultural formation in generosity was from the living examples of others. Certainly the spiritual insights and inspirations we encountered growing up as Christians provided an impetus towards generosity. However, it wasn't doctrine or moral laws that provoked us in this direction as much as deep personal longing, from what we experienced and what we therefore knew to be possible.

With the confidence gained from the generosity of our parents, we each went our own way, aspiring to make a creative impact on the world. Since we took our sense of generosity for granted, we matured into adulthood seeking relationships and friendships of consideration, civility and gentleness. In hardscrabble careers, we each pursued success and ambition, sometimes to excess, yet never losing hope for either personal situations or social development of more fairness, understanding and opportunity. And, later, as writers, we each gravitated to optimistic projects and inclusive themes, using language to undertake that respectful, participative exchange between text and reader. We persisted alone, on our own, with day-to-day duties, while dreaming of collaborating with others in projects of shared purpose and significance. And through all the bumps and grinds of work and busyness, we ached, each in our respective way, for beauty in our human reality, and for respite and renewal in the splendour of nature.

All this circling around generosity occurred before our first date. On meeting each other we felt an immediate sense of belonging, speaking honestly and openly with an easy intimacy that we later came to realize was possible because of our shared predisposition. Generosity was something valued in our souls, and while both of us appreciated its worth and had learned its vocabulary, neither of us, sadly, had found it in past relationships. As we began to give words to our mutual attraction, and define our hopes as a couple, generosity became the prism for our relationship, and subsequently our marriage. We committed—humbly and imperfectly—to making generosity the value infiltrating all our other values, a part of our daily living with one another, family, work and community. Over the years, we have used generosity as a filter for what has happened to us, while committing to it as an everyday practice. With time, trials, tests and triumphs, we have come to formulate some basic principles and methods for what we believe is the art of right living, of doing the right thing through generosity of spirit and of self. In this book we give shape to what we have learned.

Generosity—as the word itself connotes—is about not only giving but also generating. It is a creative act rather than a handout, an attitude or ethos rather than an exchange between someone who has too much and someone who has too little. Even when pursuing other objectives, or coming from other motivations, generosity is often at the heart of what brings peace and real self-worth. Various studies among people who buy lottery tickets indicate quite clearly that the dream of winning is actually for the "double reward," for the opportunity to share the benefits in special ways that make a difference to family or friends. Having volunteered in prisons, women's shelters and hospitals, we found that people like us who started out wanting to do something positive came to learn that we, the supposed dispensers of generosity, were in fact the recipients of reams of joy, insight and satisfaction. These experiences are signifiers for the truth about generosity, which is that it is part of what constitutes human beings as social creatures, and part of what fulfills aspirations, possibilities and innate creativity. In virtually all relationships, but especially in friendship, partnership and marriage, generosity is the expansive quality energizing hope and happiness. As such, generosity is not really optional. Nor can it be occasional. Rather, it works its uplifting magic only when it becomes a central characteristic and ordering principle in one's everyday life.

Generosity is not someone else's project to piggyback upon. It is not a spectator sport to cheer on from the sidelines. It is a personal choice about what to do, yet, more importantly, also about who to be in relating to another human being or circumstance. The responsibilities and pleasures of generosity pivot on this evolution from wanting to do the generous thing to wanting to become a generous person. This is why we have called this introduction an invitation—as a request rather than recommendation, as an opening to participation rather than as a "to-do" list. When generosity is embraced as a pillar of identity and as an attribute of personal integrity, it becomes an internal truth for constructing one's life. It is thus a source of purpose and a reservoir for meaning, which, perhaps, is the reason generosity is so common to so many religions, yet equally compelling without any religion at all. Generosity can have ramifications well beyond conventional expectations or rational beliefs. But whether its impacts are large or small, the practice of generosity reveals something inviolable about human reality. Living and acting generously certainly impacts others, but the most transformed is the practitioner of generosity, for by *being* generous one *becomes* generous. This again is the art itself, the ebb that fills and renews, and the flow that pours forth one's gifts into the waiting, needful, ever-regenerating world.

Many of society's magnanimous transformations have come about because of courageous acts of generosity by individuals who could not accept injustice or inhumanity. Personal choices, whether for compassion, resistance or forgiveness, became inducements for far-reaching social change. This is what happened when Nelson Mandela opted for reconciliation with his apartheid oppressors after years of inhuman imprisonment. This is what Dorothy Day exemplified when, in solidarity with displaced workers during the Depression, she opened her modest home to give rooms and emotional shelter to prostitutes working the cold, hard streets. This was the dream of equality and opportunity that Martin Luther King Jr. preached and lived despite the demeaning burdens of racial prejudice he had borne his whole life. Most people may never be heroic reformers on this scale. Yet in every life there are moments or situations in which injustice challenges the individual with many of the same sensibilities of what is human and right, with much the same potential for contributing change in the world.

Generosity is generative—generating change, generating opportunity, generating transformations. Conversely, most intractable problems to be faced today can be seen as involving the opposite, that is, *degeneration*—the disorder, conflict and breakdown that so often traumatize relationships, fissure communities and spark conflict.

Whether it is in the clash of civilizations, or disagreements between religions, or political fighting between ideologies, constructive dialogue is impossible without some generous opening to the other who is different from one's self.

The degeneration so painfully present in global or social realities also plays its fracturing part in our personal lives. As is often the case with family strife, differences impose divisions even with people who are loved. Fears incite isolation, especially from people who are alien or far removed, which is the reason simple antipathy or "crossfire" is preferred over conversation. Generosity, as an exercise of inclusiveness, can help bridge misunderstandings or alienation, and create connections despite disagreements. Making a common human home, personally as well as within the community, is not only a right but also a responsibility. With a generous attitude the interdependencies become more apparent and of higher priority than the disconnections. To listen to another is to be generous. To be open to others' beliefs and aspirations is to accord them the generosity of validating their lives' experience and desires. To stand with others in distress or suffering is to provide hope for some regeneration. Conflicts are not denied. Differences are not papered over. Anguish and anger are not trivialized. Generosity does not yield instant peace, harmony and tranquility. But it does keep problems from having the last word.

Generosity's rewards are contagious. Our experience as a couple is that generosity has no predictable calculus, achieving outcomes that surprise, and impacts that exceed any formula. We have been beneficiaries of unexpected receiving, and blindsided by exponential benefits that far surpassed what was imagined in our giving. Only by practising generosity can we learn its lessons and realize its benefits. As with freedom or liberty, generosity's inherent wisdom is uncovered only in its experience or doing. Generous acts beget generous responses, which means that it spreads not only the asset that is given or shared, but also the optimism that inspires it. This is not to suggest that generosity is easy, or that it evokes instant reciprocity. The joy, instead, comes from being connected to a sublime, ever-constant creative source that has flowed through human history and carries humanity into the future. As people, we are constituted to generate—to proceed, to make progress, to overcome hurdles and improve conditions—and in the process draw purpose and pride from participating in a larger cause. The reward ignites inner satisfaction that is drawn from the generative participation in the bountiful flow of life, and the grand project of making history human.

Today living generously, in its fullest sense and practice, seems rare if not forgotten. Why is generosity so rarely invoked in public discourse? Why does it feel so thin in so many relationships? And why is it so unfamiliar in many workplaces? Part of the answer to these questions relates to a basic misunderstanding that reinforces several misperceptions and leads, at least in our time, to a wholesale misapplication. The misunderstanding is that generosity is often used as a synonym for charity. As noted earlier, charity may be a part of generosity, but the impulse is bigger and the horizon wider. Charity is being moved to give. Generosity is being moved to change. With charity the transaction is giver to receiver. The relationships in generosity are interactive, and more mutually expansive. Charity is mostly a reaction or responsibility based on sympathy, while generosity is also an anticipation or imagination sparked by empathy. There are overlaps but in general terms *people are charitable with what is of surplus to them, and generous about what is important to them.* It may well take a charitable heart to be generous. Yet not all charity is generous. Giving an old coat to the Salvation Army may fulfill a need without actually affecting the cause of that need, and without generating hopeful change.

From such faulty misunderstanding it is easy to slip into misconceptions. Many believe that generosity is something exceptional, practised only occasionally and for those far away, instead of intertwined in ordinary life. One culprit here may be the way generosity is imprinted on children. One of the first exposures many of us received to the needs of the world beyond our own homes and schools was in the form of the ubiquitous UNICEF boxes that arrived for every trick-or-treat expedition at Halloween. What a wonderful expression of solidarity to have children canvass for aid to children. Without diminishing this box of hope, it is also true that the purpose of this excursion was to remember those less fortunate while collecting treasures of candy and chocolate for oneself. The implied model is of generosity as reciprocity, in that one could expect to get while also doing the good of giving. And it encodes and affirms the sense of generosity as a passing on of what is surplus or not really of use to the giver. The divide between giver and receiver is institutionalized when coins are solicited for those with not enough to eat and drink, by people collecting bags of treats for themselves. This is an example of no-cost generosity: nothing is given up when only leftover change is passed on. So, when there is no cost to being generous, there is no personal stake in the outcome; when nothing of the self is given, one is left removed from and untouched by the flow of generative possibilities.

A more adult misconception is that a generous act involves writing a cheque for emergency relief in world catastrophes. It was indeed moving to witness the vast outpouring of global giving in response to 9/11, or for the tsunami victims in Southeast Asia. These occasions prove our premise that generosity beats in the universal human heart. Still, the question that lingers is, why does it take a violent shock to the global system to awaken our collective empathy and compassion? The answer probably involves a combination of good intentions with mixed or unclear motives. Hence the paradox of phoning in contributions to people left homeless half a world away while missing the needs of the homeless in one's own communities. While it's undeniable that generosity has come to the fore, it is also honest to acknowledge that on-demand generosity, marshalled by the media and made possible through information technology, incites the world's heart while the less sensational agony or loneliness of those nearer home fails to attract the spotlight and therefore remains outside the realms of interest, involvement and wallets.

Misunderstanding generosity as "just charity," and misperceptions about what to give and what to expect back, contribute to the misapplication of generosity. Like so many other things in society, generosity has been conditioned and redefined by consumerism. Commercial and managerial logic, which has done wonders expanding the economy and raising wealth in markets, has infiltrated other sectors. Synagogues, museums and universities have "strategic plans." Churches, police forces and government departments focus on "customer experience" or "satisfaction." With this orientation towards efficiency and results, business has become the lens for "managing" even not-for-profit projects. As a result, charities too have become "products," with image and message crafted to compete for "awareness" and "purchase." Made slick by marketing, even the most pressing needs get "positioned" and packaged as products to buy. The most worthy of causes become another sales pressure as people are inundated with countless unsolicited requests for time, attention and especially money. With so much aggressive jostling for "purchase" or patronage, many people become frustrated by the intrusion of commercials, flyers and telemarketing. This sets a vicious cycle in motion. The "selling points" of generosity need to become more shrill to break through the "clutter" of so many causes. The heart eventually hardens against being ceaselessly cajoled. Even caring people become immunized, which often means turning away from some who have the greatest need because they have the fewest resources for making their "business case" in the marketplace of grief.

Sadly, generosity is regularly reduced to another commercial exchange. Treated as consumers, people more and more expect something back for their giving. Hospitals and other health foundations use high-value lotteries for fundraising, promising attractive odds for cars, homes or millions in prizes in exchange for purchasing a ticket. There is no doubt that worthy work is being done. But as with those UNICEF boxes at Halloween, the "giving" becomes muddled by the "getting." There is nothing wrong with wanting a tax receipt. Society has always commemorated donors by putting their names on university chairs, medical research wings at hospitals, or cultural centres. However, true generosity is not premised on a corresponding reward. It deserves commitment and investment in creativity whether or not there is payback and acknowledgment. When the motives or environment for giving are so drenched in the consumer currency of satisfaction and return, people risk missing the generative connection with those whom they are hoping to help. And they can be left as suspicious of the motives of those in real need as they are of those who incessantly market to them. Generosity as consumption achieves some productivity and efficiently raises money; however, it often feels as exhausting and empty as shopping in crowded malls on the last days before Christmas or Hanukkah. The intent is a good one, yet the experience does not really qualify as the art of right living because all the buying does not satiate one's vital need for expressing what is heartfelt.

When generosity is a give-and-take with a bottom line, it is frequently reduced to more of a financial than a human commitment. It becomes a quantity: "This is how much I gave." What gets forgotten is the quality: "This is what is necessary and possible; this is what is fair, liberating and human." With growing consumer debt, there is for many less and less "quantity" to invest in what matters to the heart. Guilt can raise its ugly head when real needs overwhelm capacities and resources. Sometimes despair and disillusion kick in when issues calling for care and attention become too daunting or depressing. Others give up on giving because they are unsure whether their offerings will actually find their way to those in need, or suspicious that what they give will get lost or wasted in bureaucracy. The marketplace keeps up the pressure, commoditizing causes while also appropriating "generous terms" to keep the consumption ball rolling. There is "zero percent financing" for purchasing new cars, and "don't pay" events for buying furniture. Ironically, this market generosity is rarely applied to true generosity. There are never zero percent micro-credit programs for struggling farmers, or "don't pay" holidays for single-mother artists, or entrepreneurs in urban ghettoes.

Consumers expect to get what they pay for, which is not the right premise for generosity. Mother Teresa taught that it is not how much one does or gives that makes the difference, but how much love is put into the doing and giving. Any simple act of giving, motivated by the intent to make a difference, can therefore have generative consequences far greater than the actual amount donated. It is not that money does not matter. The key is that money be placed in service of the priorities of the heart.

As a couple, we have experienced generosity as life altering because it involves so much more than merely "giving." The most serious and obdurate challenges to our own integrity and beliefs have often, in some way, required us to trust the process of generosity even more—not necessarily giving more, but giving into it. We have learned, by trial and error, that recognizing the nuances of generosity does not come easy, but experiencing it as a much grander source, to both draw from and contribute to, has helped us define its art.

This introduction is entitled "Invitation" exactly because the forces of generosity are not always comfortable and kind; they require change, consistent hard work and courage. The attractions of generosity are incessant yet it remains a personal, conscious choice whether or not to respond to its summons. In this time when the economy is ever more tightly interwoven, and when the natural ecosystem is so fragile, all decisions and behaviours have consequences affecting human destiny. Nothing can be regarded as completely neutral. The smallest breath takes in all that the world produces. The shortest drive to the mall sends out carbon that burdens the earth. Within this interdependence what is done—or not done—is latent with responsibility as well as opportunity. One can choose either to be impervious to what furthers disintegration, or to embrace a generative alternative. Generosity that is imposed is like freedom that is forced—a contradiction in terms. It must be embraced, chosen and lived, as a response to its bidding.

Mahatma Gandhi famously remarked that there is enough in the world for everyone's need but not enough for everyone's greed. This is, in part, the reason we have written this book, because we consider generosity a prerequisite for problem solving, and therefore not to be approached casually. We will share the issues and challenges that have arisen as we have opted for generosity over absence, for involvement over dismissal, for stepping into situations of need over pulling ourselves back into comfortable forgetfulness. We have not always got it right, but as the years have passed, we have become better at recognizing generosity's subtle, yet transforming, lessons. And we're still learning.

The exploration begins with reflective personal time, preparing to see anew in order to comprehend what is required to change, to enable and express generosity in all its variants. There are guidelines for becoming more generous and advice for maintaining a generous attitude. There are also examples of how these ideas have come alive for people, with the lessons learned by them. As generosity is at the heart of life, and evident in all religious traditions, the study of generosity would be incomplete without some examination of its intrinsic spirituality. And, there is a summary of how to practise generosity every day, and create a consistent environment of happiness and hope.

Preparing for Possibilities

GENEROSITY is a type of wisdom, a mix of knowledge, experience and love. Like any wisdom it must therefore be both desired and sought after. Invariably in such searching, generosity meets the seeker. This chapter outlines how to be ready to respond to generosity's invitation.

Already beyond what we know—and what we can even imagine—generosity flows as part of the momentum of the created universe. Every human being surfs on waves of unexpected grace, inheriting creative possibilities that reach farther than an individual's life, and yet are not beyond that person's capabilities or talents. It does not take a religious perspective to be cognizant of this expansive reality. Nor does it contradict a scientific mindset to appreciate the abundant, wholly unmerited generosity by which every being is born and sustained. Creation may be invisible or taken for granted, yet it is there, precious and indispensable in the air to breathe, the food to eat, the water to drink, and the natural resources to craft shelter and tools for making a living. Accompanying this abundant natural reality are the smaller, intimate and conscious generosities that allow us to function within creation: the delicate courtesies that keep our relationships respectful; the opportunities of recognizing one another's claims for dignity; the rights and privileges of being seen, heard, counted and accounted to. Busyness has frayed many of these courtesies, but such etiquette is indispensable to the social trust needed in communities, companies and countries to deal with the complex problems of our time.

Generosity is to be considered as not only an ideal, but also an essential need for everyone.

Whether it be expressing love or receiving it, participating in friendship, striving to realize some longed-for opportunity, or creating understanding, the wellspring for these manifestations likely involves some generosity gained, given or realized. Optimists see the glass as half-full. Pessimists see the glass as half-empty. A generous perspective sees the glass as a container for sharing and the water as a gift from life. Generosity is an attitude as well as a characteristic of action. To begin preparing for this wisdom, it is vital to know what you need on a profound, interior and intimate level. Learning how to be generous to others means first learning how to be generous to yourself.

Generosity is, in essence, a virtuous act in that it has to be practised to have any impact at all. Virtue is recognized when valour is applied to righteous ends. Fourth-century theologian St. Augustine of Hippo described virtue as "the ordering of love." Augustine challenged the prevailing perceptions about virtue as a hard discipline of duty, by instead relating one's best behaviours and most worthy habits to those that relish and create possibilities for others. Such ordering is an act of "relation" that consists of "enjoying what we should enjoy and using what we should use." To be virtuous is, therefore, to be responsible, being alert to what is required and being ready to act in response to that understanding. Virtue exists within a person's character and comes alive through consistent, loving action. It is, as Augustine stated, "the art of right living."

Generosity depends on the practice of virtue for three reasons. First, as a form of wisdom generosity is realized only in action. It gains its strength through constancy and not by being learned as a theory. By Aristotle's definition, practical wisdom is "truth in the service of action," not for one's own benefit but for "what is right and honourable." One needs to pause to be clear about personal motives and discern how one's choices serve others and express love. This orientation to others is the core of generosity.

Second, as generosity will challenge the easy comforts and assumptions considered normal by the status quo, it is essential to prepare for criticism. There are downsides, risks and undersides to all choices. No heart is perfectly pure and no need is unambiguously noble. However, with virtue, it is possible to develop a foundation for standing on principle, and for weathering the opprobrium one faces for daring an unconventional approach to life's problems. We must not kid ourselves: practising generosity is often criticized or unwelcome. To frame a generous response to a labour dispute at work is a threat to the existing power structure of the organization. The same is true with simple courtesies. Letting a car into your lane on a crowded highway often raises the ire of those immediately behind you. It is common to laud the value of virtue in the abstract and dismiss it in the everyday. Yet part-time goodness almost always withers before it sprouts.

Third, being generous is like physical exercise. It is not only good for you, but also indispensable, as all human life is naturally intertwined with generosity. Yet it is elusive unless it is embraced with commitment, working out its muscles, gaining strength through the consistency of a balanced regimen.

Generosity then can be understood as a virtue comprising many virtues, a harmony of capacities and talents that, when exercised together, aids perspective and abilities. St. Francis of Assisi taught, "Those who possess one virtue will possess all the others, provided that they do not harm any of them. A person who hurts one of the virtues offends all of them and does not possess any of them."

From our experience and study, we have found ten virtues that, when nurtured and practised together, inspire and give form to the art of generosity. It is by comprehension and living of these virtues that generosity flourishes.

COURAGE:

Courage means being strong of heart. It is to dare, and to strive for, what validates human hope. One needs to be courageous to break the shackles of the status quo, especially when it feels familiar and comfortable not to expect anything better. It takes courage to admit the truth, and then act on it to create better possibilities for self and others. Courage is generative in that it helps create the conditions, or secure the circumstances, that serve what is right in life. Dignity, artistry and freedom are all understood to require taking risks to achieve or accomplish. While these outcomes may also require fortitude and sometimes bravery, it is courage that underlies the creative ability to change.

Any effort at personal growth, whether shifting attitudes or deepening self-knowledge, entails vulnerability that can be faced only with courage. Life's most trying issues—like leaving a job, ending a broken friendship or relationship, or challenging the dominant culture—involve taking risks and facing uncertainty to satisfy the restlessness for something better. His Holiness the Dalai Lama stated in his book *The Power of Compassion* that people become more courageous by being more altruistic, as it is compassion that ultimately feeds our inner strength and increases our determination. With charity the aim is often to make up for a problem, to compensate for some unfairness or tragedy. With generosity the conviction is more creative, to actually solve the problem and risk breaking what is dehumanizing so as to unleash more just and dignifying opportunities. This courage to change what is wrong in the world hinges on the courage to also change what is wrong inside one's own heart.

DISCERNMENT:

The more seriously one embraces generosity as an attitude or approach to life, the more deliberate one must become about where to invest creative effort and generative commitment. Discernment is a form of personal evaluation and judgment by which one looks beyond the normal decision-making factors to consider more authentic motives and more meaningful implications. For instance, while one *chooses* what to do, one *discerns* the why—the underlying principles and beliefs that are expressed not simply in one's actions, but also, more tellingly, in one's habits. With discernment we also discriminate, so we are opening to the truth of a situation more than merely assessing its facts or apparent reality. In many ways decisions are made about exterior things, while discernment reveals more of the interior motives. Decisions usually involve some weighing up and contrasting of the relative merits of options. One discerns by seeking richer understanding from the honest and evaluative criteria of the heart.

Generosity can very easily be wasted or abused if it is practised only in reaction to whatever gets asked of us. Discernment is central to the capacity to set priorities. This means choosing not between good or bad, which is still fairly straightforward. Rather it helps one differentiate between those tougher choices involving a lesser and greater good, or between a lesser and greater wrong. Practising discernment as a virtue requires developing and trusting one's intuition in order to know which is the right way to be, the right thing to do (or not do). Intuition is that visceral intelligence available to us all, that reacts to a situation before thoughts or thinking impose their rationale. There are likely many reasons behind those moments when we toss change into the hand or hat of a homeless person. Many of these feel spontaneous and indeed involve intuition. With discernment, we connect these random acts to the needs and ideals of our own hearts. And we link small or seemingly unrelated opportunities for giving or receiving into that larger trajectory of a life lived in a generous spirit. If your motivation is love in the service of others, then it is wise to discern whether your actions will be for this reason or could be predominantly to please others, to appear to have good manners or for reciprocity.

Ongoing discernment is necessary not only for self-understanding but also to appreciate what the world needs most and to effectively direct one's own particular talents, skills and time. Discernment connects actions in the moment to one's basic principles and desires. It prompts us to be creative, to immerse ourselves in generosity's expansive possibilities.

HUMILITY:

To be humble doesn't mean being a doormat. Nor does it imply automatically responding to everyone's needs as they emerge haphazardly. Humility, instead, represents an honest sense of proportion. This sense of scale and connection is vital because without humility giving can all too easily become an exercise in power, while receiving can all too often feel as if one's dignity is diminished. Generosity is an interaction of creative potential, not power. It takes humility to give freely, with no strings or demands attached. It takes humility to give what is actually needed instead of what we may want to give. And it takes humility to give without expecting public acknowledgment. If we are not humble, then the supposed generous act can be more about us than about the reality requiring transformation.

Humility seems passive and unassertive. Yet it takes strength and resilience to tame the ego, and its sometimes mistaken presumptions. Society places ever-greater importance on self-esteem. Humility does not negate the valuing of self; indeed, it accentuates it by placing this worth and potential in the proper web of interdependencies that none of us can deny, yet ego sometimes forgets. We have to be humble when discerning generosity because usually something much bigger than ourselves is at play. Viewing a clear starlit sky in open country reminds us of how minuscule we are in the big scheme of things. We can never presume to be the originating source of generosity. We can be only its conduits.

Humility invites us to help others without selfish ambition and to look to others' interest rather than our own. Practising humility is to be sometimes invisible in your giving so as to avoid the desire for gratitude, acceptance or reward. One famous writer, a titan of twentieth-century literature, chose to send money anonymously to a young writer of talent who was struggling beginning his career. A few years later, the younger writer, growing in public stature, gave his unknown patron's newest novel a scathing review in a national newspaper. Despite the irony, the successful writer stayed true to his generous principles and continued to send money to the unaware, and still needy, recipient. As in the *Tao Te Ching*: it is because the way of the heart never attempts to be great that it succeeds in becoming great. This greatness is not about boosting pride and ego but about contributing, as one can, to the greater good of others.

COMPASSION:

When true feelings are honoured as the requirements of one's own integrity, it is inevitable that the heart opens to the reality of others. In almost all the great religious traditions this inherent capacity is called compassion. More than calibrating return or odds of success, we have to be able to be moved by others' stories and needs. With compassion, we imagine from the heart what it means to be in the place of another. This is not just empathy, which means to share feelings. Nor is it only sympathy, which means feeling pity for someone else. Compassion is a form of solidarity with the joys and sorrows of others. By being passionately united we end up sharing the passion to live and learn, sharing the aspiration to dream and create, sharing the humanity of grief or mourning, sharing the wonder of celebration or hope. Compassion is central to generosity, because it stretches us out of complacency or self-absorption. This receptivity to others binds us across differences and makes us capable of extending love. Without compassion there isn't much sensibility. And without compassion we get caught in the reductive exchange of plain give-and-take. With compassion, generosity's aim and impact are on multiplying the possibilities of standing together.

MERCY:

The fact that generosity is so peripheral in our modern world is, in large part, because the value of mercy has been diminished or denied. Most of us live in an economy and culture that are premised on give-and-take as a function of merit—you earn the rewards that are justified by your efforts. By implication, people who are in positions of want or disadvantage can easily be dismissed as somehow being responsible for reaping what they have sown. The rush and busyness of life, and the fear that many people experience, have contributed to the hardening of our collective hearts. It is within these economic pressures that we can look on those in need as if they have somehow created their circumstance. Millennia ago Aristotle warned that people who do not feel the vulnerability of others are culpable of hubris.

Mercy is the emollient for softening such judgments. A merciful person is not only moved by someone else's distress, but also feels a need to offer consolation that assists or makes a difference. With mercy we walk gently on the earth— gentle-men and gentle-women—and extend courtesy and care, not for manners' sake but to engender civility and dignity in the public domain. Such kindness recognizes our shared kind: that we are much closer to each other despite our differences, and interconnected as souls so that everyone deserves heartfelt consideration. Instead of pity, mercy offers a reordering of the situation so as to alleviate distress and recover the possibilities for happiness. Sometimes our language gets in the way, so that even wanting to help fails to bridge the chasm of experience and perception. This has happened with society's shift from offering "welfare" to expecting "workfare." Generosity is expected to be efficient and to be merited. While creating job opportunities and ending systemic reliance on social assistance are worthy goals, the terms and underlying presumptions impose another arbitrary judgment on someone else's situation, categorizing in ways that depersonalize. Language leaked a hardened mercy also in the way that the aid bureaucracies came to refer to the displaced from Hurricane Katrina as "refugees." We know from friends who live in Louisiana that this label was frightening and demeaning to the displaced, because it seemed to imply that they came from somewhere else. The threat to identity and dignity—which the storm victims suffered and to which all of us can relate—was from loss of home.

Mercy is always about giving others the benefit of our doubts. As with compassion, a healthy mercy, with lack of judgment and with sympathy from the heart, is fine-tuned as we practise it towards ourselves.

RELIABILITY:

So far, the virtues of generosity are fairly obvious, involving outreach and concern for others. Less apparent, but equally efficacious, is the practice of reliability. Pronouncements or beliefs count for naught, without trust that actions will be constant and followed through, after commitments are promised. For generosity to thrive, reliability matters. This constancy doesn't mean that you can be expected to always act a certain way—or be willing to be available for all that is asked of you. Rather it means that each of your *ways of being* is continually generous. Reliability is the concrete quality that brings good intention to life. Beyond practicality, reliability is generous in and of itself because it allows people who know you to thrive in the confidence that their needs, expectations or contributions will be respected.

Predictable generosity can feel counterintuitive; however, its very reliability serves as a key factor in achieving order, whether societal, in community or for a creative and functioning personal life. Both of us have learned that a hidden pillar for intimate and lasting relationships is, without a doubt, being reliable. It provides stability, not as a passive assurance, but as a stronghold for one another's vulnerability and as an enabler for growth. Constancy is vital in practising generosity as it is the way we earn trust in our relationships.

TRUST:

American political scientist and author Francis Fukuyama calls trust our "social capital." To be involved in a generative relationship always invokes trust. You give without being able to control the outcome. You receive without being able to ensure full payback. In this gap of unknowns, we trust that the generous thing is nevertheless the right thing. As it happens, the depth and quality of trust depend, in large part, on the depth and quality of generosity. In our research, we discovered that trust becomes magnified by aspiration. We allow trust to grow by making and then living up to a promise. The more idealistic the promise, the more augmented the trust. This is why trust is like having generosity in the bank.

When we can more fully trust each other, we can entrust our generosity to others, and then we can trust others' generosity to us. All sorts of possibilities and commitments are engendered by such trust. Trust is generative, as it also creates the elasticity for mistakes to be made, forgiveness to be given and received, new opportunities to be ventured and risks to be taken.

HOPE:

In our hard-nosed focus on pragmatism, hope is often discredited as a dream or wishful thinking. But hope is essential for imagining what is possible. At its core, all generosity is an act of hope, because without hope there would be no expectation that being generous would have any effect at all.

- Hope assumes that the way things are will not be the final or definitive state.
- Hope motivates risk for achieving something better.

- Hope is the reason to give to those in need.
- Hope is the reason to receive what is offered.
- Hope provides confidence—that anything done from a generous heart or through practising any of the virtues of generosity will actually make a difference.
- Hope denies cynicism.
- Hope dismisses suspicion.
- Hope inspires beauty.
- Hope promises a possible future.
- Hope is optimism practised with intent.
- Hope fuels the fire of love.
- Hope expresses everyone's most basic aspirations.
- Hope generates the agitation that stokes progress.

REMEMBERING:

Jewish philosopher and scholar Avishai Margalit tells us that what we remember is what we really care about. Today, it is easy to forget, or not even consider, one's own history and its defining art and ordering culture. The stories and lessons that mould our meaning and identity are lost between facts, dates and numbers. No single narrative can capture the sweep and struggle of history. However, remembering not only recognizes the truth in the past, but also sets the terms for making sense of the future. If we remember to look back, we may be able to interpret the present. Recollection is critical to consciously recognize personal acts of generosity within the course of our own evolution and spiritual development.

Remembering our history and culture requires us to recall those people whose actions have exemplified exceptional generosity and had remarkable consequences in changing views, as well as lives, for the better. There are historical examples such as the bravery of Polish priest Maximilian Kolbe, who at Auschwitz offered himself as a substitute for a family man who was about to be executed by the Nazis. There are current examples such as a group of concerned American women who, with Kathleen Price, founder of Mission of Love, descended upon New Orleans a week after Katrina, to offer food, medicine, clothing, massage and footbaths to police and emergency workers, who most had forgotten were also in need. And there are personal, humble models, such as

Arturo Dalla Costa, an Italian immigrant to Canada who, as a night-shift labourer, used his days to drive other immigrant men to construction sites to get the work he had struggled alone to find. Remembering and honouring generous lives teach valuable lessons about today, while upholding their contributions that made possible a more generous future.

BALANCE:

The final virtue—necessary for all needs—is the balance experienced from regular rest, restoration, listening and just being human. Caught in the everyday rush, many of us seem to be always on the brink of exhaustion. Our ever-greater busyness takes all the energy we have, leaving us little to give to what really matters. In the unconsciousness of always being rushed, we can easily fall into the opposite of generative living. Enslaved by duties or ambitions, we can end up denying ourselves the very time and reflection that provide us with the necessary balance of peace and joy. Rushing can cloud our perspective and limit our possible offerings to others. It seems a paradox that by not taking regular, disciplined rest, we undermine our opportunity to deepen generosity in ourselves; our families and communities; and our work, minds, bodies, souls and environment. Yet this "taking" of time for the balance of rest and activity is what creates the surplus to be reliable in our giving to others. A generous balance—to be received so that we can give—includes at least one day a week when labour is eschewed, and diligently taking a proper annual vacation, instead of the occasional long weekend.

Withdrawal from work and rest once a week is the true meaning of Sabbath. The creation story from the Bible's Book of Genesis explains that God called forth creation, and after doing the heavy work over six days, God rested on the seventh. Sabbath was such an important part of this creation story that it was made part of the Ten Commandments, given by God to Moses and the Israelites as they wandered the Sinai Desert after their escape from slavery in Egypt. Hardly discretionary, the Sabbath is the antidote to slavery; it breaks the cycle of exhaustion— even exhaustion from generosity—by allowing us to recover, rest and renew after exertion.

Sabbath is required to prevent succumbing to ceaseless doing, to recreate, to take stock, to go through the discernment that allows us to know where to invest our energies the following week. To be caught up in continual productivity—a common practice in a world that values multi-tasking—often results in burnout, which, paradoxically, then requires more than just one day to recover from.

We two have experienced that the day off a week need not be Saturday or Sunday, as there's a need for flexibility of choice. It can be any day within the seven. The task is not necessarily to become religious but to be religious about taking a break! People are not automatons. They are human beings, and productivity alone does not define humanity, nor does achievement or success satisfy the human soul. People need free time to experience freedom. They cannot generate, or be regenerative, without resting, nor can they be open to receiving what is generous towards them if stuck in a perpetual rush.

If all these virtues feel like a burden—something to master, something else to do—then the most pressing generosity may be to first practise them on yourself. Take the courage to say "no" and rest, to discern what you need and desire. Be compassionate towards your own stresses, fears and hopes; be merciful about your mistakes and shortfalls. Trust (as the mystic Julian of Norwich wrote) that "all shall be well." Hope by remembering those you wish to emulate; honour your own needs for peace and balance. As you begin to widen your perspective towards yourself, you are, in fact, already developing some preliminary skills of generosity and right living.

The Risky Business of Changing

With slowing down and taking stock, you begin to live a more balanced life, and open yourself to the call to be more generous and more attuned to the creative possibilities around you. As in any growth, a change in attitude or in life situations is almost always required. Reality continually changes and shifts, yet we are inclined to get caught in a reversing frustration of pent-up desires—being stuck for wanting more. We may want change, yet we also want it to be without cost. This is understandable as change involves upheaval and uncertainty, while familiarity is a safer place to stay. However, even if this familiarity is destructive, making us ill, depressed, withdrawn or despairing, we are all too inclined to cling to it, as if truth and transition for healing were the real threats. Strange as it may seem, generosity begins to flower in change, and change itself is often the most generous gift we can offer. Restlessness for change begins with a small voice within—usually a voice one would prefer to ignore, a voice that can be deadened by submitting to ever more activity, a voice lost in addictions to work, alcohol and television. Believing the effort to change is too extreme, we commonly devote far more resources and energy to whatever we need to do to avoid the truth that is emerging. But, as the wisdom of our bodies and souls reveals, truth is guaranteed to emerge even when we would prefer it go away—and invariably this truth, this call for change, works its way through our bodies and our emotions sometimes in the turning points of illness, or unforeseen personal "tragedies." Whatever it is, we come to recognize this truth when it arrives; when it can't live any more trapped in the status quo.

Once upon

⌒

THE STATUS QUO

She had been a professional woman, never married—she liked her independence. Now she was a senior, she'd outlived most of her friends, and had never contemplated reaching eighty-five. She suffered severe pains in her knees and was afflicted with an insistent cough. She couldn't go out without her walker and now that winter had come, it would not be wise . . .

A neighbour suggested she move into a retirement apartment, something she could afford, with a nice view. She could take most of her furniture, even buy some new pieces perhaps, and there was a doctor on call just by pushing a buzzer. All meals were prepared, too.

It would be best, she thought, but as the day approached she lost her nerve. Better to stay in the old place; the move would be too much for her. She just couldn't, not at her age. She didn't want to disturb her neighbours, but shopping was well nigh impossible. Would they mind picking up a few things next time at the supermarket? Don't worry about me, she'd say, but they did worry, all the time.

And so she continued to exist, without changing. After a while she fell in her bathtub, breaking her hip, and was transferred to a home. Everything was done in such a rush that she had no time to pick the pieces she wanted to take with her. A friend had the whole lot—including her furniture—bought by a jobber. Now she felt more homeless than ever.

NB: Change comes whether we accommodate it or not. However difficult, the most creative possibilities are usually realized by embracing rather than resisting change.

Change can be the doorway for entering generosity because change, in itself, is a generous act. Protecting things as they are is the reverse of generosity, because it usually involves fear and clinging that can hurt, and never provide healing. Changing, following what is known to be true, even without surety or guarantees, is committing to a personal regeneration, which, in turn, generates other possibilities.

Change is invariably unwelcome at first. We are all creatures of habit, but change *is* generous for insisting that something better *is* possible. And with personal change, we also enrich and liberate those closest to us, the community in which we live, the company for which we work, our friends and members of our families. Our courage to change *always* enables others to be courageous to change. The discernment to pursue what matters most allows others to also cherish the truth for themselves. To be generous by changing liberates others to change and also regenerate their lives.

Once upon

A PLACE

It had stood for over eight hundred years, a tall edifice, built of rock gathered from the nearby mountain stream. Now empty and desecrated, its windows broken, its walls faded, its floors littered with filth, it had lost its former glory and become a hideout for randy teenagers.

She had wanted change; she was ready to escape the interminable cycle of deadlines, the constant screech of city sirens and pressured expectations. One day, as she was flicking through magazines, she spied the advertisement. She called the phone number, bought a plane ticket and said a prayer.

As she walked over a carpet of violets and listened to the song of the birds and the rushing water, she knew she had found home. This was peace. She made an offer—the money would come, she was sure. Some called her courageous—giving up all and moving to a foreign country—but to her mind she had no choice; the decision had already been made for her, all she had to do was step in.

She wanted to make it a centre of pilgrimage again, just as it had been centuries before. And so it became, a place filled with such grace and abundant gifts that she has stopped counting . . . and the pilgrims keep on returning . . .

NB: We must risk change to follow our bliss and truth and destiny—however illogical. This generative act inevitably links to something greater, enabling others' bliss to also be ignited.

Changing—inside and out—requires consistency, fortitude and boldness. When you begin to actively change, you open yourself to truth, and thus open the generative capacities around you. Exposing yourself to something new introduces newness to the sphere you influence and depend upon. Being flexible brings refreshment to all you touch and do. Such change requires honesty, and a strong will, because it usually upsets the lives of others, raising uncomfortable questions that frequently stir up others' unconscious desires for change, which causes backlash and even resentment. This invariably happens in the least likely of places and people. Your friends, who have always supported you, may start teasing or making comments that imply criticism. Colleagues at work, who have come to depend on your predictability, may respond negatively to being threatened by the example of change. Both of us have taken choices vital for the needs of our own souls only to be called callous, selfish or irresponsible. The truth is that these responses are, undoubtedly, not from real friends, but from friends of the status quo. What is usually meant is, "We like you the way we have you, even if you don't like what you have," or "Don't do what we know we have to do because we can't," or "Don't turn my world upside down by changing; I have enough stress hanging onto what is," or "I resent you stirring up what looked like a good thing."

There is not much you can do to respond to these sentiments except remain consistent in your steps of change, holding onto what we have discovered to be three vital principles in the process of conscious regeneration:

1. You cannot please everyone, and trying to do so will actually be ungenerous to everyone, including yourself.

2. You will please so many more when you have completed the process of changing, because that renewal will inspire others to also take risks towards what they most need and truly want.

3. Giving up on renewing change for yourself once you have started is often a betrayal of generosity in that something necessary and creative has been stunted and undone. In fact, you have not only hurt yourself by not completing what is necessary for your growth, but also deprived others of the benefits of insights and inspiration for themselves.

Jesuit writer Anthony de Mello wrote, "On the day you cease to change you cease to live." It is wise to remember that one's whole life is about continual change. Life never stands still or stays the same. Being comfortable with our lot is a fallacy. We are always called to grow. Generosity is conscious change, an investment in what we hope and need to become. If this latency is left unattended, you will, in effect, be caught up in a momentum that is not yours, taking a route farther away from the direction of your life's purpose. If you ignore change, you ignore generosity. If you resist or depreciate generosity, you essentially resist and depreciate the unequivocal imperative to grow and change, to mature into a whole human being.

PRACTISING GENEROSITY IN CHANGE

When you start to consciously practise generosity, it is vital to remember that it is not about giving more money, or even more time, it *is* about being more generous with yourself towards others, including those who criticize you or are threatened by your changing. The generous response to the negative reactions of others is to listen to them, to hear what it is that *they* need from your actions or changing attitudes. You must be more generous with yourself as well as honest with others, when explaining the truth of what it is you need. The clearer you are, the easier it is for others to understand and let go of any hanging prejudices or niggling reservations. The generous response to the positive support and responses received is, simply, to be grateful.

To enter the art and heart of generosity isn't about floating on good feelings, but about constructing a worthy boat ready to combat the stormy waves ahead. To be prepared is to be willing to confront what prevents you becoming truly generous; to be aware of what makes you fear change, and where you are inclined to inflexibility and perhaps cynicism. Do you need time for your heart to heal?

Generosity creates the spiritual, as well as personal, ability to change and regenerate. For people with faith, God has proffered abundant generosity. The natural world is not only proof of a divine generosity but also enables us to deepen our spiritual relationship with creation. People who do not believe in God usually recognize that they stand within a network of gifts and graces that pass to us unmerited, yet warrant us to pass on to others. Generosity could well be the virtue upon which the world—and for many of us, the heavens—thrive. Generosity is a cog in the wheel of creation. Changing ourselves to become more generous helps us experience how this generosity of creation can fuel our way. Becoming generous enlivens partnership with not only each other, but also, in spiritual terms, with the Divine.

TWO

Widening the View

───
───

EVERY year for twelve years we have looked out the windows of our summer home onto a beautiful field of wildflowers. The alfalfa plants renew and return every year, offering a vista of green leaves with purple flowers amid yellow and white daisies, and providing a refuge for hundreds of butterflies. We thought ourselves blessed indeed. A woman visiting us last year, a medicinal herbalist, casually walked the perimeter of the field and said that we had twenty-nine healing herbs growing wild on our property. What we thought were weeds, she explained, were leaves to heal burns or insect bites. She pointed to other plants that could be turned into teas for assisting digestion, or for helping cleanse the liver or relax the prostate. There were also flowers and stems for restorative baths. Through her expertise, we came to recognize a rich variety of edible plants to add to salads that are high in vitamins and minerals. Instead of a pasture we had a pharmacy! This hidden wealth was not only in diversity, but also in the unexpected gift for healing and well-being. It was there for us, even as we missed it. It was there as an offering, even if we did not fully appreciate its worth.

Our guest had more surprises to share. Coming upon a stinging nettle, one of the few plants we warily recognized, she knelt to the ground and, while explaining its medicinal properties, gently began to stroke it with her fingers. The stinging, it turns out, is not automatic, but happens only when the plant is threatened by an unconscious intrusion or aggressive act. In her hands the nettle was a treasure to be caressed and appreciated. How many other things that are feared and shunned, we wondered, hold similar hidden benefits? What other experiences in life that had left a painful sting could have been treasure troves had we had the sensibility to unlock them with a caress? It is a matter of not only seeing, of course, but also trusting that what is known does not exhaust what is possible. Another surprise from our guest came from her explanation about the healing power of herbs. She described the medicinal values in terms of relationship. Rather than tell us how to pound, pulverize or prepare herbs, she spoke of readying ourselves to be open to what the herbs can give us. Potency resides in the willingness as much as in the chemicals; in the meeting and interchange rather than the actual dosages. Not surprisingly, the generosity of nature teaches much about generosity among people—that it isn't necessarily about preparing to give more but preparing to receive more fully all that is on offer. The process is one of immersion in generosity, rather than some new angle of personal mastery.

As with our field, most individuals do not have to go very far from home to achieve a widening view. It is often in what you are doing, where you are living, whom you are agreeing with or arguing against, that all the mystery and questions of generosity come to the fore. In the daily reality of work and families, there are already possibilities, like herbs, to heal and make us whole, if we are prepared to receive them. In friendships and interactions, there are choices, as with stinging nettles, to either caress what is fragile and beautiful or be left scratching and irritated for being unconscious of what is really needed. This chapter aims to help one see anew, to recognize what may be invisible for being so near, and what is especially precious within the familiar.

THE FOUR MOST GENEROUS WORDS

This widening view begins on the frame of four modest words that may well be the most generous in our vocabulary. The first two go together as "thank you." The other two couple in "I'm sorry." As words common to everyday use, they are a reminder that generosity is far more pervasive than is usually thought. Both sets of words involve double consciousness—an inner or retrospective sense of self, and an outer regard or respect for another. Both also involve some appreciation of what is due to one another. Gratitude is a response of owing back to the one who has given. Apology is a response of owing back for some deficiency. Much more than some auto-response politeness, "thank you" or "I'm sorry" gives an explicit reality to a generous attitude. No relationship can ever operate on perfectly balanced reciprocity; indeed such clinical equality would likely be deathly boring or emotionally numbing. Relationships always involve some disproportion between ebb and flow or give and take. "Thank you" and "I'm sorry" acknowledge the asymmetries, not to harden or take the imbalance for granted, nor to muddle receiving with just taking.

"Thank you" appreciates what is received and honours the giver. "I'm sorry" appreciates the one to whom the apology is offered and honours the one who committed the infraction. Both phrases restore, creating trust and goodwill for a relationship to grow. Both therefore generate and are life-giving, adding impetus and momentum to moments that otherwise, through the absence of generosity, can hurt, create misunderstanding, and breed atrophy and isolation. It is not that we give or receive on a scale, wanting gratitude or apology for all our actions; rather, a generous exchange completes what is unfinished, reconnects what is fissured and uplifts what is possible in the future. "Thank you," said from the appreciative heart, enlarges the heart of the other. "I'm sorry," said from the contrite heart, heals the heart of the other. Either way the benefit enriches the relationship.

Anthony de Mello wrote, "You sanctify whatever you are grateful for." Offering gratitude recognizes the effusive spirit inherent not only in generosity but in life itself. For people who believe in God a simple prayer of "thank you" effects, even without great reflection, an immediate connection with the deeper wellspring of the Divine's graciousness that undergirds all human potential. The more thankful we are, whatever our beliefs, the more we become attuned to the wondrous nexus of giving upon which we can stand and function. Nothing in creation is neutral. Whether DNA is admired as an elegant outcome of natural engineering, or as a design reflecting the love and brilliance of a divine creator, we are, in the end, all gifted beneficiaries of this fundamental dancing spiral of life. Life is not simply a mystery, but a mystery of enabling and sustaining largesse. Light and water are gifts, as are oxygen and food. As we partake of them and remember to offer our gratitude, then every "thank you" lays bare our fragile yet wonderful relatedness. Every "thank you" calls us to witness the beauty and bounty our everyday eyes often fail to see.

When gratitude is received you feel recognized at another level of your being. Something you've given or done has been noticed, valued as making a difference, is—in however minuscule a way— celebrated. More than mere acknowledgment, something springs to life within when you receive a heartfelt "thank you." It is like planting a seed that bears unexpected harvests. And it reverses the pain of receiving nothing. It is not that people ache to be on pedestals but they do ache not to be invisible or dispensable. Especially in relationships when one's generosity goes unnoticed, something within can shut down. Desire to offer more gets sapped; the willingness to risk anew is stifled. Withholding—or forgetting—thanks contributes something much graver. Instead of regenerating giver and receiver, it destroys the sacredness of the act itself; instead of giving and celebrating life, it dismisses and degenerates, exacerbating isolation and withering love.

Once upon

⁓

A TAKE

His best friend's son was getting married, and he offered to help with the reception. He was an excellent organizer and did not mind doing the odd jobs behind the scenes that freed the family to just enjoy the occasion. That would be one of his gifts.

Expected as a guest, he willingly became one of the servers. As an insider—yet not one of the busy family—he was the "go-to" guy for others working in the backroom. Musicians came to him for help with extension cords. He found himself dealing with the rental companies, and even heaving chairs and tables into new positions as the design of the room came together in the final moments before the party. He helped the waiters when they needed it, cleared the tables after the dinner and was there late into the evening.

When toasts were made and thanks extended he was forgotten. And when pictures were taken with family and friends, he was left out. "So be it, things happen," he thought as the festivities ended and people streamed home. But as months passed and no words of gratitude were offered, he began to feel as if his gift had no value, or more truthfully, that he himself—and his friendship—didn't matter.

NB: Most often, it is in the small details of courtesy that generosity counts.

When times are hard and full of suffering— whether from illness, shock or stress—gratitude often wanes before need. Sometimes, what you have is not what you want, so the impulse is for restless-ness or resentment rather than thanksgiving. What is essential in such distress or disappointment is to keep your heart malleable, honestly attending to what you need or hope for while truly valuing what is possible. Gratitude does not wash away agony or grief, which are real aspects of our human experience. Nevertheless, it makes the agony or grief bearable or meaningful by generating connections that live on beyond us. We know of heroic people who have faced their own death being generous to others, staying open to thankfully receive from those around them, in large measure so that consolation and healing are available to all.

A friend of ours was given a few months to live after having suffered breast cancer for many years. Doctors had suggested a hospice for her to spend her last days in, but she would have none of it. She went home and was cared for by her husband and sons, knowing that it would be a challenge for them but wanting especially her boys to have the experience of caregiving, and the memory of being indispensable to her. Rather than commiserate, she organized a sewing group of women friends, who, along with her family, made bags for collecting coins that could be distributed for those in material need in her native Sri Lanka. She died with a familiar smile on her face, assured that her lifelong work taking care of others would be continued by those who loved her. Generosity such as this almost guarantees that loss and grief are a passage rather than a permanent state.

"I'm sorry" is certainly the relative of "thank you." All of us at times make mistakes. As humans, we naturally suffer from inadequacy and imperfection. At some point, either when conscience tugs or when time has revealed an uncomfortable truth, we come to contrition for generosities assumed, forgotten or mistreated. "I'm sorry" breaches the breach—reaches across the gulf created by our unconsciousness or selfishness—to affirm our indebtedness to each other. Just as "thank you" recognizes a gift, "I'm sorry" recognizes a rift. Both sentiments involve a movement of giving and receiving. When you say "I'm sorry" you are inviting forgiveness of another. "Fore-give" can be to give ahead, give forward, to give in advance, to give before the reciprocity is rebalanced, to give restoring wholeness to a bruised or broken relationship. This too is a grace, often radical in its ramifications. While we give forgiveness, we recognize that we are all equal in fallibility, that none of us has a monopoly on being right.

An honest apology is risky. "I'm sorry" initiates an admission of fault that requires both the humility to take responsibility and the vulnerability to be wrong. Generosity diffuses hurt or wrongdoing when the transgressor gives up his or her self, exposing the truth about the situation without assurance that this offer will be accepted. In this way, there is always a learning for the contrite individual. Admitting to wrongdoing gives us a chance to reflect on its root causes. For the person receiving the apology, the contrition provides relief that truth has been expressed and heals the wound caused by the rupture.

Not every "I'm sorry" is wrought with life-altering consequences. But every apology is a stimulus towards making things right, together. Forgiveness shared not only heals the past but also becomes an investment in the future.

Once upon

A TIME

She'd suffered polio as a child and always walked with a limp. One day, while waiting for patients, she heard a knock on her surgery door.

"May I come in?" A familiar face from her past—it was her primary school teacher. "I need to say something."

"Please sit down."

Her teacher pulled a kerchief from her pocket as her eyes watered. "It's been many years and a lot has happened. One of the biggest events is my daughter—she has cerebral palsy. Every day I'm as challenged as her!" They both smiled, fleetingly.

"It's been on my conscience and when I saw you in the wards of the hospital yesterday, I took the opportunity . . ." They waited. "I need to apologize—to say I'm sorry."

"For what?"

"For the way I did nothing while the children mocked you in class—I'm ashamed."

"I can't remember," she answered, politely.

"I can't forget," the teacher said, "especially as I suffer with my daughter through her own trials and affliction."

"Thank you for your words."

"I hear you're a wonderful doctor."

"I try."

After the teacher left, she buried her head in her hands and sobbed with relief and gratitude.

NB: It's never too late to say you're sorry.

When an apology remains unspoken, it contributes to the existing injury. To not know to say sorry suggests a hard-headed resistance to learning lessons. To know the fault and not say sorry is a form of cruelty. Either way, a calloused heart blocks compassion, and denigrates the other's dignity. Many of us increasingly assume a "no fault" attitude that makes us not only immune to culpability but also aggressive to any suggestion of deficiency. Rage and anger flare from this—the violent stridency that comes so easily from always being right and never being in the wrong. If we do see something amiss in ourselves, we are inclined to explain away the sting of culpability. Excuses are found to justify lapses in discernment or behaviour. Self-love, it seems, means "never having to say you're sorry." Rather than confront or correct what has been wrongly done, we reverse the logic to shine the light on ourselves as victims, or blame others or circumstances as the cause.

Apologies in this mode are often earnest yet insincere, more about the plight of the perpetrator than the injury to the one impacted. Self-absolution degenerates quickly to self-obsession. There is not only no reconciliation, but also no personal growth. Nations play this game to deadly effect: Japan refuses to apologize to Korean "comfort women" forced into prostitution during the Second World War; Turkey refuses to apologize for the Armenian genocide in the aftermath of the fall of the Ottoman Empire; Canada refuses to apologize to its indigenous peoples for literal and cultural abrogation of rights and treaties. Silence or denial mars the present, not the past, perpetuating the indignity, stifling justice, stunting growth in collective understanding.

At the other end of the spectrum are the easy apologies that often involve politicians or celebrities making appearances on television chat shows. These are acts of contrition as performance art, using the fusion of news into entertainment to put the best spin on wrongdoing. As a

PR exercise, this form of "I'm sorry" follows the clever script prepared by lawyers and marketers. Usually there is firm and outright denial of the accusation, as U.S. President Bill Clinton made with wagging finger about allegations that he had had extramarital sex with a young intern. As the evidence mounts, there are attempts to disqualify the source or sully the injured parties. Only as the facts become incontrovertible does the person, celebrity or company finally come clean. If the PR counsel is sophisticated, then the act of apology will include some demonstration of remorse, lessons learned and rehabilitation, such as sessions with various clergy members to explore the tortured soul. Not to say that these people are not sorry in some way, but such stage-managed coming clean does not honour the trust that has been ruptured. If anything, cynicism has grown more acute even as the scripted apologies have become more public. Since the aim seems to be to recover reputation rather than restore relationship, the conclusion is often degenerative rather than regenerative.

Learning to say "I'm sorry" involves the same sensibilities and skills as for "thank you." In fact, these four words exercise and bring to fruition all the key virtues of generosity explained in Chapter One. It takes an open heart and a strong heart— *courage*—to offer gratitude or contrition. It takes *discernment* to identify whether a situation warrants thanks or an apology. It takes *humility* to accept being beholden to another, either for the obligation of generosity received or for accountability for mistakes. It takes *compassion* to feel remorse for hurts imposed. It takes *mercy*, not just tolerance, but real empathy towards others and towards one's self. It takes *reliability*, which means constancy and consistency, in voicing appreciation and in following through with actions that prove the lessons from forgiveness have been integrated. It takes *trust*—wanting to increase it, wanting to repair it, sharing in its reciprocities and responsibilities. It takes *hope* to see gratitude and forgiveness as aspects of a prodigious pattern of interconnected belonging and becoming. It takes *remembering* to take neither for granted. And it takes *balance* to recognize that in any relationship "thank you" or "I'm sorry" is no one's exclusive monopoly.

THE MORAL CHOICE

That generosity is defined and expressed through not so much a single action as a mode of being is proof that generosity is an attitude. It is a disposition of a heart filled with gratitude. Acknowledging, and benefiting from, the innumerable gifts and possibilities that are available to us, we are also charged with the responsibility of sharing them. Workplace surveys consistently find that most people wish for jobs with meaning, and suffer frustration if productivity displaces all other opportunities for significance. People thirst to make a difference making a living, being generous with talents and energies in ways that have benefit beyond the economic arithmetic of any project. It is usual to feel we have more to give, and that we deserve more than some sustaining minimum. Gratitude recognizes these possibilities and promotes their unfolding.

No doubt there are challenges and obstacles to this grand economy of relationships and opportunities. But, in many ways, the challenge is to see what is already there, and not to miss—as we did with our wildflower field—the gracious qualities underlying human life. Human beings are conceived through an exchange of intimacy between parents; they survive by drawing nourishment and opportunities from countless other contributors to the necessities of life; and they participate in their rights of freedom and dignity through the obligations and duties of others. Few people can survive in isolation; no one can really thrive in his or her humanity if removed from the tidal flow of life's enabling gifts. To open ourselves to the fulfilling possibilities available to us carries a corresponding moral responsibility. Almost every choice has moral significance because not everything we have and not everything we decide to do is purely merited by us. Not every duty or debt we owe is ever fully discharged. Indeed, the most precious inheritances, such as peace or freedom or opportunity, are also the most fragile, requiring us to nurture them, to invest ourselves in the responsibilities that renew what we so richly profit from.

We can choose to ignore the invitation to be consciously involved in this exchange of gifts. We can choose to mine the benefits of countless generosities in our life without inconveniencing ourselves to make commensurate offerings towards the sustainability of the whole and the future. But as choices, such turnings away are not neutral expressions of preference. They are not casual in intent, nor isolated in their impact. To stand apart from generosity is always to hurt it, for it breaks the chain of interconnection, and flouts the reliance on one another that none of us can escape.

Widening the view of generosity means seeing with our hearts. It is from this visceral capacity that moral moments are recognized. There's a sympathetic pull, a queasiness at another's distress or misfortune. Our minds may do the analysis to best determine what is working or broken, but it is our hearts that provide the early warning signals that something is morally amiss, unjust or ethically at risk. Sometimes real heartache is overwhelming, causing us to turn away from the images of suffering from the all too frequent calamities that strike our world. But usually the call of the heart, in a moment, reveals more subtle sensibilities. This call comes when ideals push and prod, and when principles compel action. The accompanying restlessness, or frustration about injustices, is a positive expression of our hearts' desire for what is right.

We tend to think of morality as prohibitions or precepts for not doing harm to one another, for choosing right over wrong, and good over evil. The great spiritual teachers promulgated such moral laws, but as a means rather than an end in themselves. For Buddha, the Eightfold Path was a method for living with compassion. For Moses, the Ten Commandments were a structure of rules for living in freedom after enslavement, and for accepting a covenantal relationship with God. For Jesus, love of neighbours, including those who are one's enemies, was the means for achieving peace on Earth. Morality requires a system of rules but only comes alive in its practice. Indeed, too tight a reliance on rules or too rigid an interpretation of compliance often creates the very inhumanity or exclusions that morality aims to correct. Generosity is the yeast that brings moral dough to rise—it is the spirit that goes beyond the letter of the law, thereby asserting the priority within moral precepts of what is generative, what serves life. Through moral choices we not only discern what is right, but also make the investment of self and commitment to work it through. German Lutheran minister and writer Dietrich Bonhoeffer (killed in a concentration camp a few days before the end of the Second World War) described this generous priority of obligation as "being free for others." While addressing a church group, Lilla Watson, a young aboriginal leader in Australia, said, "If you have come to help us you are wasting your time. If you have come because your freedom is bound up with ours, let us work together."

Perhaps because technology continually promises improvement in the future, society operates with a certain moral amnesia. Part of what seems forgotten is that generosity has been the inspiration and prerequisite for many of the human, social and economic rights that most people now consider their due. As self-interest has been the ordering principle for the economy, it has been adopted as a driving value for society, and thus for many individuals. This reinforcement of self-interest means that generosity, by default of its aims and ethos, is on the sidelines of social discourse, and also seems somehow spurious. Hence the irony of runaway self-interest. Focusing only on what is personally wanted has so stifled individual capacities for generosity that many of us have ceased knowing how to give ourselves the time, peace, belonging and rest that *we* really need. Compartmentalizing generosity does not so much narrow our engagement with others as narrow the scope of the freedom and fairness we are so desperate to receive. When the immorality or amorality around us becomes the reason for closing down our own generosity, we end up suffering an individual as well as social breakdown, a crisis of heart as well as of culture.

THE GOOD PERSON

A common refrain when discussing morality is to hear others describe themselves as "good people." Both of us have grown wary of such disclosure. Do they mean that they subscribe to particular truths of morality, or simply that they do not intend harm to others? Often it seems that what "good people" implies is that by comparison they possess certain qualities of judgment—that they are not as mean, acquisitive or without scruple as others. Perhaps they also mean they support precepts for world peace, the preservation of the environment and fairness in the practice of human rights. While these sentiments seem generous, they are, in fact, usually quite superficial. Claiming to be a good person rarely has a cost to it. The more adamant one seems to be in self-proclaiming goodness, the less reason exists to examine motives, morality and desires, or to confront personal growth. Paradoxically, this easy claim to goodness often conceals a much deeper fear of what is wrong or iniquitous. It is a passive-aggressive attitude that by refusing self-reflection fails to plumb our complicity in what we each owe in gratitude or apology. Being "good" is therefore the ready excuse for not changing, for resisting what morality requires, in the illusory comfort of who we already are.

The rule of thumb for spiritual development, acknowledged by all great religions, is that if you claim it, you are not it: if you claim wisdom, you are not seeing your own foolishness; if you claim enlightenment, you are missing your own darkness; if you claim goodness, you are blind to your imperfections and facility for injuring another. Even claiming openly to be a generous person carries a risk of exposing the opposite. Management teacher Jim Collins observes that "good is the enemy of great." His point is that nothing undermines potential as much as complacency. In moral terms, the state of "goodness" is the *consistent* practice of generosity. It is in offering ourselves to the challenges of what is good that we become moral. It is in advancing the goodness that serves others and renews community that we receive goodness. Being a good person may be a good starting point, but in the end it is just not good enough.

In summary, generosity is goodness where it counts—which is always in action for others. If we hold back being generous, we inevitably hold back doing something good. This is the moral choice. History teaches us that doing no harm is all too often a harmful act that allows patterns of oppression or malfeasance to go unchallenged. At its best, doing no harm is a false measure of goodness because such neutrality denies the investment in love and care that we need to make towards one another to counter the wrongs that exist in life and society. Only when we generate hope out of despair for people around us are we participating in the movement of goodness. Only when we help raise others to a state of equality have we fulfilled the debt imposed by our own rights and privileges. Again, with generosity there is no neutral ground. Generosity always takes sides. By its action it defies what perpetrates or perpetuates harm.

Widening one's view of generosity, therefore, does not require more data or knowing more about the world, but knowing more about oneself. In experiencing gratitude every day, as we give and receive it, there is a wealth of inherent learning. So too with the experience of apology: what one is sorry about, what one feels sorrow over, what hurts and creates personal remorse, holds the revelatory wisdom of generosity's call, and its much-needed possibilities.

THREE

A Symphony of Three

THERE are two degrees of generosity. The most prevalent is as a one-way linear process, from giver to recipient. Less common is the more organic circular form of generosity that has three mutually enhancing qualities: giving; receiving; and circulating. The difference between the varying degress is significant because in the three-part dynamic, generosity shifts from being an isolated action to become a form of participation. Everyone is involved in making this the music of the heart, experiencing the back-and-forth inter-play, which individuals simultaneously contribute to and enjoy, whether as giver or receiver. The three parts, however, are not separate or sequential. Instead, giving, receiving and circulating are interconnected possibilities that together give form to the artistic essence of generosity. Later chapters will be dedicated to each quality separately. For now, we'll explore the interactions of what make up this more fulsome and rewarding generosity of the collective and creative heart.

"Giving" and "receiving" are already accessible concepts. Less familiar is the idea of "circulating." Circulating changes everything because it implies that generosity exists within and beyond any single decision or action. Consider bees and flowers or butterflies and blossoms. The giving and receiving are mutual, yet the generative consummation of new life occurs only within much wider circulations. No one is the originator, and any generous act is part of a continuum. This more expansive view of generosity as a system or synergy is both state of the art and ancient.

Scholars rightly call this time one of paradigm shift. For centuries science and the process of understanding were based on Newton's theories, which essentially ascribed mechanistic properties to the physics of the universe. With Einstein all that changed. Rather than fixed structures observing immutable laws, Einstein formulated a new basis for understanding reality as the dynamic relationship between energy and matter. Physics is not the most generous field of study to draw upon, but, to summarize, Newton saw the world as a finely crafted pocket watch while Einstein saw it as a beach being continually re-formed by the interplay between water and sand.

Some are inclined to apply a Newtonian perspective to generosity, with giver and receiver in some "mechanical" exchange of "properties." However, "circulating" very much represents the new paradigm in which generosity is unleashed as a reforming "energy" in "relationship." Adapting systems thinking to generosity, we can see that it has its own gestalt and spiritual ecology. More than a simple, or singular, transaction between giver and receiver, generosity is actually an ongoing relational commitment.

Even as cutting-edge science relentlessly uncovers lessons for understanding the beauty and fragility of systems, the appreciation of inter-relationship actually echoes the more universal wisdom of our religious traditions. Taoism is premised on a fundamental dynamic complement between yin and yang. Jewish mysticism recognizes the divine presence as both within our material world and withdrawn from it as *tsimtsum*. And Christian doctrine envisions a single Godhead composed of three persons as Trinity. Dogmas obviously vary, but these and other religions share a perception of reality based on a flow of love and creativity. Scientific minds now appreciate reality as involving networks and ecologies, with nodes of information and dialogue. Spiritual minds, such as French paleontologist and priest Pierre Teilhard de Chardin, perceived a similar unity extending to all matter and consciousness.

If systems terminology is fairly new, "giving, receiving and circulating" is, itself, an ancient practice. Cultural anthropologists have uncovered evidence that societies based on matriarchal values often functioned as economies of circulation, rather than of competition or direct exchange. Some who have been studying this phenomenon call it "the gift economy." As writer and researcher Genevieve Vaughan observes, ancient societies in which the roles of mothers were especially valued practised a more communal balance between abundance and prosperity. Modelled on the intimately observed lessons of Mother Nature, these communities, by combining kindness and fairness, achieved sustainability and harmony from an intuitively systematic generosity. Such priorities for circulating stand in stark contrast to our current economic, religious and political systems, which are based on more patriarchal or masculine values of achievement, status, accumulation, merit and winning.

To even consider the ethos of this new-ancient circulation is a challenge, for it reverses many of our most cherished—or most entrenched—values. When the priority is based on circulation, giving has more worth than earning; receiving has more power and dignity than buying or consuming; and circulating has more benefits and advantages for community than return on risk, or reward for investment. While a feminine trait and a matriarchal value, this capacity for gift giving and receiving is not reserved to women. It is part of what Carl Jung described as the anima, the complement to animus—the yin and yang that reside in each individual's consciousness, within the bodies and psyches of both men and women.

Writer and laparoscopic surgeon Dr. Leonard Shlain introduced a complementary theory about the collective anima in his book *The Alphabet versus the Goddess.* With his doctor's understanding of the workings of the human brain, Shlain contextualized the current movement in history as one in which culture is moving from left-brain dominance to right-brain *prominence.* The overdeveloped rationality of specialized work, linear processes and fixed text is giving way to a more inclusive, image-oriented and emotional sense of flexible interconnection. Information technology, especially video, is changing the way our brains process information and form impressions. This is a far-reaching change, one that may well take generations to establish, yet it represents a basic turning away from the competitive and exclusive sense of "divide and conquer" to the co-operative sensibility of "create and unite."

Shlain's theory, along with the teachings of Jungian writer Marion Woodman, inspired a few women friends to organize and stage an international conference on the emerging anima. To give proof to the theory, as well as to give practice to their own convictions, the women decided to use the "giving, receiving and circulating" paradigm to actually manage every facet of the event. Each had left the business world in search of healthier ways to make a living. They now set out to be generosity entrepreneurs, beta-testing their principles through a venture called The Anima Conference. The idea was to contribute a new view, and share the lessons from working within the three-part cycle of more feminine (or generative) economics. Their purpose and desire was to plan and create a conference as an exemplar of this alternative way, and to not only cover their costs but also generate profits to circulate anew.

Global in their experience, these women were used to thinking big, so they invited sixty speakers from all over the world to present over four days. With twenty volunteers on their organizing committee, they experimented with meetings, agendas and practices, to create operational methods of giving, receiving and circulating in each and every interaction.

For example, the practice of giving became the imprint for *how* they met. Instead of launching into a "to do" list with a chairperson at the helm, they began with a common prayer and silence to bring the group together. They always sat in a circle to share authority and be equal in presence. Each person was honoured by being first invited to share her ideas, feelings and insights about herself, her work, her life, the challenges and changes happening to her, before contributing her particular organizational expertise.

This often took most of the meeting time, but was anything but unproductive. Indeed, the last thirty minutes were so energized from the inclusiveness that decisions were made quickly and unanimously while responsibilities were naturally assumed. After everyone had been heard—had been given to—there was always ample time to quickly and unanimously arrive at common intent. Unlike a traditional brainstorming session, which seeks to extract thoughts and ideas, the circular process provided a type of heart-storming

that brought out the best in the people involved—
including their best ideas.

*NB: People flower and achieve great things together
when they are welcomed and received as who they
are. Creativity flows from the security of being surrounded by the hearts of others. Collective truth
springs forth easily when idividuals are embraced
and invited to share in a circular form.*

A second commitment towards this experiment
in circular economics was in practising appreciation. Applying two of the most generous words,
the group took the time to say "thank you" to each
member, for what she was doing, and for how she
was doing it. When someone risked personal honesty, or disclosed some uncomfortable truth, that
person was valued for bringing forth something
precious with the group. Others present were, in
effect, receiving an offering that deepened the
conversation and therefore generated other possibilities. In the rational world of facts, truth is often
used like a hammer to pound home a point or to
win an argument. In the relational circle, truth is
the gift that sets others free.

NB: To see and hear people for who they are is to receive their uniqueness and their gifts. This experience always liberates possibilities for circulating what has been learned in the encounters, including respect and trust.

The third reform was to choose circular symbols and inclusive language. To avoid defaulting to old-fashioned hierarchies and competitive habits, all words derived from warfare or battlefields were avoided and substitutes explored. This proved challenging, especially with common project management words such as "deadline" (a military term meaning a prisoner would be shot dead if he crossed a particular line). Experimenting with new vocabulary was part of the circulating. The group tried "arrival" and "intended time," eventually coming to consensus on "timeline" as the code word for fulfilling mutual obligations. Another problematic concept involved the "targets" for fundraising. The group reimagined the whole fund-raising process as the rings of the interior of a tree. The metaphor now was one of organic growth, so that over two years of planning they could consciously work out from the centre of the circle.

NB: Even though we have become more sensitive to gender exclusion in our speech, it is also necessary to recognize how sports and military terms perpetuate a distorted competitive paradigm. "Beating, winning and losing," "aiming for targets," and "shooting for deadlines, spearheading projects, rifling through material," even "strategies for success," are everyday words premised on "me" versus "you," or "us" against "them." Words matter profoundly because they order our worldview, and give reality to what we expect of—and owe to—one another. A more inclusive world awaits words that give name to the circle of interconnection, infiltrating our processes and perspective with generosity.

Once upon

AN OVERFLOW

He was looking for work in their city. He'd been having a hard time. Life hadn't been easy for the couple either. Things had been financially tight; Christmas was busy, with a house full of grandparents and all the children at home. Although they both were tired of cooking and providing hospitality, he was a special friend and welcome to stay with them.

After he'd gone they discovered the card he'd left. A few heartfelt words of gratitude and a wad of cash, far more than a hotel would have cost him. They couldn't accept this—it was too generous—but it would insult him to return it. The money could pay the overdue bills. What an unexpected gift!

A week later they learned of an unemployed single mother who needed a new furnace. With little to spare themselves, they bought a furnace for her. She too couldn't believe their generosity, and they explained what had happened to them. It wasn't long afterward that they heard that their unemployed friend had landed a job, and they were happy to inform him how his generosity had spread full circle.

NB: From giving out of emptiness, the guest and his hosts were filled with hope. So much so, that much more was circulated, benefiting not only the giver and receiver, but another in the circle, who would undoubtedly give in turn. Generous acts almost always abound and circulate in unexpected ways, contributing change, and spreading the advantages for all involved.

A fourth habit for the Anima group was to be proactively generous, extending care and attention in hosting the sixty speakers, as well as the hundreds of ticket holders who were attending. This anticipatory service was inspired by the "Simple Prayer" of St. Francis of Assisi, which advocates "not so much to be understood as to understand." The organizers took it upon themselves to stand in other people's shoes. Empathy became the basis for setting priorities. As speakers were giving their time and their wisdom, they were to receive not only compensation, but also comfort, care, privacy, honour and respect. The hosts were merely circulating gifts that were already being offered and relished.

NB: Speakers and guests said that they had never before attended a conference where so much care had been provided, so much so that most needs were resolved invisibly and in advance. People were so overwhelmed by what gave proof to love, that many donated their fees to help with the conference's parallel project—to set up a women's health clinic in Kabul, two years before 9/11 made Afghanistan newsworthy in the West.

The fifth practice in living up to circulation involved attention to the flow of money. The organizers had borrowed to pay the start-up costs, and as the ticket sales began, many who wanted to attend couldn't afford the fee. In the spirit of giving, receiving and circulating, those who needed help were invited to give what they could afford, and others who could afford more were invited to help make up the difference. Surplus flowed to cover deficit; those in need received, while those who could give made their own connection to the animating spirit of the conference. In this free-form circulating, dignity was enhanced for all, with community being created far before the conference began.

NB: In the patriarchal model, all activities are aimed at profit. In the generosity circle, the surplus is generated from needs met in relationship.

The sixth and often most difficult aspiration was to live in the organizational flow of surrender to the form of giving, receiving and circulating itself. As the conference's theme was to discover the anima forms through the feminine spirit of motherhood and balance, conventional expectations of what the result would be had to be given up and given away. Like any act of generosity, this involved taking risks. Grounded in the economics of the feminine, and sustained by common prayer, the conference not only became an inspiring experience for all, but also has lived on for years since, regenerating in unexpected ways and spawning small communities and projects inspired by its concepts. These included a few women helping other women in need on their street through giving, receiving and circulating. One woman, Carol Mark, bought a building and opened a gallery where artists could display their paintings, and have the opportunity to give a portion of their sales to grassroots

causes. The end of the conference marked only
the beginning as what was received moved into
larger circulation and spawned giving anew.

*NB: The experience of practising generosity in
the three-part symphony proved, to everyone
involved, that a matriarchal economy is more
than an idea; it is a practical, ancient yet new,
and unique formula for problem solving and for
creating sustainable community. This approach
can live, operate and succeed within our current
reality provided we have the courage to seek alter-
natives to the harsh realities of competing for
rewards by merit.*

THE SECOND MOVEMENT

Authority and power in governments, religious
institutions and businesses are usually dispensed
through hierarchical pyramids. This Newtonian
gearing means that the levers of control, and the
benefits of controlling, are concentrated firmly
on top. The anthropology of matriarchal communities suggests that the pattern for exercising

authority tends to be more circular, with dignity and belonging distributed more equitably. Rather than cascade from the top, the resources and privileges are shared horizontally by everyone nearer the ground. Within the energy and relationship of this system, the motivation for generosity starts from the priority of what is needed, rather than from the availability of what is surplus.

Part of what undermines the currency of such systemic generosity is that our society values what is produced more than what is created. Women's work of motherhood remains undervalued, sometimes to the point of impoverishment, and a liability to careers in most professions. Not to discount, or diminish, fatherhood, generosity as a circulating dynamic actually demands that we revalue, and better appreciate, what is human and biologically generative—a retrieval of motherhood as the prototype of value. Examples of micro-credit extended to women in the developing world have illustrated that a small amount of generosity through unsecured cash loans enables women to make a living. Neither a handout, nor a conventional risk-based loan, micro-credit makes a profit as an outcome rather than as an objective. The driving purpose is hope for the future, allowing women to hone skills, maintain their dignity and contribute to the economic vitality of their own community.

As most of us know from experience, the motherly model of giving is not based on competition, or a calculation of return or reciprocity. It is a daily, unexceptional yet invaluable act of generosity in circulation. The economic impact and outcome will be in the growth of the child, in the talents, skills and hearts of the next generation that will circulate onwards and outwards. Motherly generosity is a gift that keeps on giving.

Although it might seem far-fetched to imagine changing our system based on merit economy, the basic premise of mutual generosity as encoded in giving, receiving and circulating was, in fact, practised because it was practical. Collective self-interest has been elevated to a virtue only in the last few decades of growing consumerism and me-generation philosophies. In the past, throughout history's trials and errors, most cultures and religious traditions cautioned against such individuality as eventually compromising our shared and limited resources, which environmentalists now call our "commons." Despite our present knowledge and economic smarts, the destruction of the commons—such as our fisheries, forests, arable lands, and sources of fresh drinking water—is accelerating. All too tragically our legacy is imperilling future generations. We are caught up in the economy of competitive self-interest, which normalizes excess as a natural, personal aspiration.

Perceived as an ideal and not a familiar tried-and-true practice, giving, receiving and circulating seems utopian and therefore impractical. As it happens, it is our existing model of production and consumption that is proving impractical. We are stuck on a treadmill of growth above all else, and current expectations of "progress" are behind the gravest of humanity's problems, including global warming, resource destruction and unsustainable development. A startling graph in a business magazine illustrated that it would take five planets the size of Earth to provide the resources, raw materials and environmental capacity to bring the whole world's population up to the Western standard of living. At a global gathering of business leaders, officials from China declared that their country would *not* be one of the leaders reducing greenhouse gas emissions. Attending the same conference, the prime minister of India declared that people in the developing world had the same right to produce comparable pollution and waste levels as producers and consumers in the world's more advanced economies. It's a fair point that if we are not equal in restraint, then we share equal rights to be irresponsible. But it just shows that pursuing the status quo is not so much common sense as common suicide. We cannot simply compete our way out of the excesses that excessive competition has created. Nor can we simply throw ourselves into new technology hoping that innovation will undo the grave risks to sustainability that technology itself has bequeathed. Not changing is the ultimate impracticality because it starves the system of the giving, receiving and circulating that we all need to survive and thrive.

Once around

A SQUARE TABLE

They sat around the boardroom table—the two male consultants with the host of female executives. The men had been employed to provide strategic counsel for a government's initiative to coordinate and integrate the delivery of social services to women. A new organization had been created with a stellar board exclusively composed of women, not only experts in the field but also lawyers and activists who had been pushing for more coordination and improved practices appropriate to women's unique needs.

After a process of consultation, which included interviews with all board members and key experts in the field, the two men proposed a radical new organizational model to reflect the obvious and needed feminine element. Instead of the usual top-down hierarchy, the consultants recommended a circular wheel-like structure. The idea was to share authority and information so as to place decision making as close to the woman in need as possible. While the technology allowed for such a system, the women in authority were unwilling to cede their overall control. Rather than adopting a circular model of operation, they opted to maintain the old directive approach that had already impeded progress on women's social development.

NB: Even people with generous aims who are trying to correct the dysfunctions of a top-down pyramid often end up captive to the power structures that block the very innovation they are trying to generate. We need men and women willing to embrace ancient wisdom while experimenting to generate inclusive and sustainable systems.

To change the future, it is necessary, as discussed earlier, to be open to radically changing ourselves—our minds, behaviours, decisions and presumptions—to foster hope in the face of destruction, and to promote aggressive collaboration in a constrictive atmosphere of winning and losing. Generosity is the key to such change, the effort, energy and ethos that enable circulation. Again, remembering that generosity is generative is vital—that it not only addresses needs or emergencies, but also creates conditions for other human-enhancing opportunities to be productively unleashed. To only take from our Earth and each other, without a reciprocal relationship, is neither morally right nor sustainable. Giving—to give and enhance life—needs to become the priority for personal, social and economic well-being. As we recoil from the threats and destruction of an aggressively competitive model, it is important not to fall into the trap of stepping from one ideology to another. Embracing a more circular and inclusive approach, although one based on matriarchal principles, is less about gender than about committing ourselves to a way of living and making a living based on inclusion, acceptance and generosity. This is not to politicize generosity or entangle it in gender arguments, but to situate generosity in our bodies, recognizing the birthing of life as a contributive element of our being human.

Once upon

A DOMINO

She always wanted to write, and when recovering from breast cancer tried her hand at a novel. It was about a woman who found hope out of the experiences of illness. The manuscript was rejected by many publishers but her husband lifted her spirits by offering to pay for its printing, as an anniversary present. They decided to give all the proceeds from the novel's sale to other women who needed help while ill with breast cancer. Then a few friends and colleagues chipped in: an editor gave her expertise in memory of a friend lost to the disease, and the designer, herself a cancer survivor, also gave of her services. Over one thousand copies were distributed in informal ways, through women's groups and by others who gave them away to women in need.

The first $1,000 in sales went to a sick woman undergoing chemotherapy while living in her car with her daughter. With winter on the way, she was able to use the gift to rent a small apartment. This began a cycle of renewal and healing for her. In a few months she was organizing workshops to help other women living with cancer, and has since become a teacher and seminar leader spreading the message of giving, receiving and circulating. She received what she needed, and turned this into an offering that she now circulates and expands to others hoping to give or receive.

NB: From sickness and rejection, the writer gave of her imagination. She received empathy and support from others who wished to share in her efforts to do something for women. When the books were received by more people, they circulated them to others. The money from the sales was then given to other women with less, who by receiving it were able to improve their circumstances and go out and circulate their own talents and skills to enable others.

Giving, receiving and circulating is not just an economy for organizations; it can offer a personal method for change in attitude and actions. The mechanical economy, and the assumptions that drive and determine so much in our society, trap many in the habitual manner of generosity, with its non-relational and exchange component. Even when people are authentically pulled to be generous, this ingrained belief causes many to ponder what it is they will be getting from—or out of—an interaction. A common attitude is, therefore, not "What can I give?" but "What will you do with what I give?" "What does it cost, and what am I getting back?" Calculation prevents circulation. This approach leads to conditional giving, with its accompanying suspicion, and prevents any opportunity for real generosity to flourish. Instead of a chance to give—of self, time, money, gifts and ideas—there are, instead, standards of performance that overwhelm any honest means of dialogue or relationship.

Black-tie charity events are more evidence of the level of extravagance that has been growing dramatically in the good cause of soliciting participation and opening wallets to those in need. Is it irony or some indicator of moral disconnection that hundreds of thousands of dollars in door prizes and silent auctions (in ballrooms with bands, during nine-course gourmet meals) are required to raise money for the homeless, battered women, children on the street or addiction rehab centres? The food, venues and social interactions are provided so participants feel good and special for doing something that is good and special in and of itself. This flow of giving can be seen as going the wrong way. People mingle with people from their own social milieu, and rarely, if ever, meet the individuals they have come together to help. The fundraising is effective, yet the circulating is stunted.

Even in volunteering situations, where a person gives time for the good of the other, he or she needs to evolve towards the economy of giving, receiving and circulating, to avoid falling into the trap of tit-for-tat exchange. All too often, people say, "I want to help," or "Tell me what to do," as they wait to receive an invitation or inducement, or instructions, before making a step towards giving. If this non-relational or reactive mode of exchange is chosen over pursuing opportunities to give, then invariably not enough is received to pass on and circulate. It is like only taking, and as a result, the transaction is ungenerously finished.

Once upon

⌒

A BIRD IN HAND

She'd earned her good reputation as a travel agent. She was known to be thorough in finding the best deal for the least cost. When a client recommended her services to a young woman on her first trip to Europe, she graciously obliged, as she always did. The woman had been on sick leave from work and this trip was a gift from her father to celebrate her recovery.

The agent found her an astonishing deal, but it had to be ticketed within forty-eight hours. The young woman questioned the price on the phone. "Believe me, it is better than you'll ever get with a regular charter," the agent answered, as the phone lit up with other calls. "Let me know ASAP, will you?"

"I need to ask you some questions. I need to tell you about my predicament. I don't have a lot of money and can't spend it all on the ticket or I won't have any to spend while I am in Europe. Could you find something cheaper?"

"Not as a direct flight. You'd have to stop once or twice and connect with another flight into Europe."

"Oh I don't think I can do that—I wouldn't know how."

"It's easy—you'd be OK." Her secretary was standing at her desk signalling to her.

"But if I do that—the cheaper way—I can't go direct, you said."

"Right."

"Are you sure?"

And so the questioning went on and on and on. Exhausted and overwhelmed by her pile of messages, the agent said, "Goodbye," and was never asked to make the booking.

NB: Not seeing what we receive turns us into disrespectful takers. This unawareness exhausts the giver, who tried to bring a caring dimension to her professional conduct and was left feeling worthless. The recipient neither realizes the benefits nor expresses gratitude. Instead, by only expecting more, she loses what is already on offer and puts an end to the circular possibilities.

⁓

We all function within a system of presumptions, attitudes and beliefs. The challenge of giving, receiving and circulating, imagined as a circular system, is to bring awareness to whether our own beliefs and actions regenerate or degenerate. Are we contributing to life, or are we exhausting it in the endless and lifeless method of get, take and hoard? The viability of any system rests not on theory but on day-to-day practice, making the music in three parts. To explore and fully understand these parts, we have to first immerse ourselves in a reflection on giving.

FOUR

Giving

THE company had been taken over. Employees were apprehensive as they waited for the executive who was being dropped in to oversee the operation. They were asking themselves the obvious: "What's going to happen to our jobs?" The new manager had led the integration of acquisitions before, and knew that the biggest challenge meeting the employees for the first time was to overcome fear and create trust. Knowing that actions speak louder than promises, she led with generosity. Upon arrival she announced an immediate 5 percent pay raise across the board. Anxiety dissolved into enthusiasm, and worry about security gave way to optimism about what would be possible together.

Giving is the foundation for sharing. It is about extending time as well as money, offering help to others—sometimes spontaneously, sometimes for the long term. It means giving gifts to those we love, to friends and family; giving birth to children; giving parts of our homes to aging parents, or making other arrangements to enable them to live out their senior years in comfort. We give ourselves in developing relationships, in marriage and through our work. We give, in varying degrees, depending on our availability and in answer to a need. And yet, as suggested at the beginning of this book, many of us become worn out with what is asked of us, and stretched by what we have already committed ourselves to. Our stress involves the very real desire to make a difference but often without the compassion, mercy and sensitivity towards ourselves that are prerequisites for sustainable generosity.

To overcome a sense of depletion or to protect

yourself from being overwhelmed, it is best to review your past habits and presumptions in giving. This requirement to take stock before giving again is to ensure that what you are doing—or giving—is honest, authentic and from the heart, contributing to the life of another, and not caught up in an inward need to feel good or more fulfilled, loved or accepted, lauded or even applauded. The virtues of *courage, discernment, humility, compassion, mercy, reliability, trust, hope, remembering* and *balance* all have expression in any commitment to generous action. It is vital to be diligently aware of when one's ego wishes to be involved in giving, and where self-pride or low self-esteem needs a boost.

The two of us each have travelled through the lessons of giving, by making mistakes and taking wrong turns. We have had regrets and made resolutions out of them. And we have been awed by the grace at work, when we have practised generosity, in varying degrees, for what we have come to consider "the right reason." Conscious action poses questions and demands clarity. We'll start our exploration with giving's default mode, which for most of us is money.

IT ISN'T ABOUT SCHMIDT

About Schmidt is a film with Jack Nicholson playing a successful salesman who loses all meaning in life after retirement. His wife dies suddenly at home, and from then on he is lost in self-absorption and unsatisfactory social encounters. While lounging one day in front of television, Schmidt is moved by one of those infomercial pleas for financial support for orphaned African children. At the nadir of emotions, he responds. He dispatches money to the child he "adopts," who replies with letters to him. This budding correspondence brings back Schmidt's sense of significance: he feels better, no longer worthless, and a somebody again from finding purpose in lifting a child out of poverty. Critics hailed the film as one of personal epiphany and to a degree it was. Yet, with a more discerning eye, it is also possible to see the undermining irony—that the greater need and benefit turned out to be Schmidt's.

Remote-control generosity seems altruistic, but the point most missed in the film was that it is not at all about Schmidt. With the giver's need fulfilled, Schmidt's giving became just another transaction, only mildly elevated above the give-and-take exchange at a grocery store. Some connective relationship was achieved, but barely enough to qualify as regenerative to giver and receiver. A trip to Africa to meet the child would have activated the courage to change Schmidt, alienating his self-absorption while enabling possibilities for lifting another in an expansive arc of giving, receiving and circulating. Schmidt could have advocated for his neighbours to adopt a school or village, or for his street to help a local family. Schmidt's money, no doubt, helped, but the point is that such giving asked so little of him, and denied him the opportunity to become active in life-giving virtue to many more people.

True givers, who know that their giving is not about them but others, also know that, by some remarkable series of events, they always seem to receive more than they gave. And they always receive much more than they even desired—or could wish for—by acting from their hearts and moving their bodies away from the security of their living rooms. The test of true generosity is whether one becomes *involved* in relationship and pays whatever it costs in focusing on the other to do that.

CONDITIONAL GIVING

We know of a young woman who works with a missionary community in Africa. In order to carry out her work—drilling wells in poor villages, helping sick and hungry children and their families, as well as serving the emergency needs of communities farther afield—she has to fundraise. Part of her duty is to report regularly on how she spends the small—but regular—amounts she receives from donors. This is, in many ways, the hardest part of her work, because of the pressure she is under to live up to donors' expectations. Even people who give little demand a lot to assuage their feelings that they might be cheated. Accountability is important, but sometimes a line is crossed when suspicion and terms of entitlement focus more tightly on what is given than on what is received. This missionary woman, who takes formidable personal risks, has to suffer insecurity and indignity from sometimes parsimonious givers, who not only keep a tight rein over how she spends the money they have given, but also contest the terms of her meagre salary, which is less than half of what male missionaries receive for the same risks and work. Such donations are more like sledgehammers, less about offering possibilities than about exacting a final return on funds. Like Schmidt, these donors have never visited to see the work at close hand, or to support what the missionary is doing with this labour. Instead, she is expected to visit *them* once a year in rounds of polite tea parties, to re-earn the privilege of their support.

This conditional giving is more common than it seems. In contributing to causes, many are inclined to want to know precisely where and how their money is spent. Not that results do not matter, but the more salient issue is that suspicion is now at the heart of much of what is given. This often cheats the moment of its meaning, and cheapens the possibilities of what is received. On the streets, too, we can catch ourselves wondering about giving money to someone on drugs or alcohol. Isn't this like pouring gasoline on a fire? The question we might instead be asking is why we need to have such control over the usage of what we give. Why do we feel we need to be absolutely sure that a recipient spends our money, or other gifts, on what we think is best? Are we giving, or judging? More importantly, if we withhold what another desperately needs, can we claim any generosity at all?

What happens with a gift is not really the concern of the giver. The only concern attendant on giving is to make sure that one's heart is part of what is offered. A friend once advised that when discerning whom to give to on the street, you simply look a person in the eye. If there is a human connection in that instant, then you can develop the encounter by asking the individual's name. In such a moment, the movement goes beyond the transaction of just giving coins to actually meeting another in relationship, seeing and speaking as human beings. Such spontaneous encounters are enriching in any moment when giving and receiving meet eye to eye. It makes magic, because invariably such givers receive more than the satisfaction of dropping a handful of coins in a cap, while the recipients get the human gift of being seen, heard and affirmed. Part of the dignity of giving money under these circumstances is to be aware that when money leaves one person's hands and drops into another's, it no longer belongs to the giver but to the recipient. This is a key lesson in giving.

When you decide to give to anyone, or anything, you are not really giving what is yours.
You do not own money or time. Both are assets
passing through in their own circular economies.
Often, things flow easily and harmoniously,
while at other times you feel as if you are
wrestling with scarcity, pushing a rock up a
mountain. We share money with those who have
less than us and time with those who mostly have
more than us. There are no conditions in such a
moment except to be present. In long-term
giving—in supporting the woman who has
given her life to helping others in the bush, or
any other worthy causes—there has to be aspiration to a generative trust that *they* will do their
best with what has been given. If you mistrust
those you give to, then it is best to ask yourself
what you are really giving. What is behind the
need to so tightly control? If it is uncertainty,
then some research may need to be done, meeting the people involved, travelling to the areas in
which they work. If your intuition or discernment is warning you from an open, alert heart,
then you need to heed these concerns. And, if
you are not clear, then it is better not to give

until you are. The aim is to get beyond conditions to encouragement: to give in ways that are not about *me* but about *us*.

Once upon

AN ENCOUNTER

He was walking downtown early one Saturday morning to get a paper, have a coffee. It was his regular routine. He always went the same way at about the same time. As he headed down the street, he saw in a distant doorway a man playing a flute. He hadn't seen this man before. As he walked, a voice inside told him to give the flute player $20. As he came closer he noticed that there was no donation box or cup—perhaps he had it wrong. Their eyes met. He was struck by the beauty of this man's face, with its slight smile. It was as if they both knew what was to happen. As he handed him the $20 bill, the flute player nodded as he put it in his shirt pocket. The flautist's dark eyes were mesmerizing. The man hesitated, but there wasn't anything more to say or do, so he headed onwards with a wave.

On his way back he looked for the man. He stayed on the same side of the street so he could encounter him in the same doorway, but he had gone. All that was left was the $20 bill, lying on the step. He hesitated—he couldn't leave it there, or could he? Perhaps he could give it to someone else? He looked around, and then he saw a bulky blanket on top of cardboard on the sidewalk ahead; a young homeless man beside a sign stating he had AIDS. The cup was empty. He dropped the money in. The sleeping man didn't wake. It was complete.

NB: Expect the unexpected. When we give, we give away ownership and certitude. By being present to what is asked of us, we have the opportunity to give where it is most needed, and without knowing how the story will end. The mystifying relationship of generosity was begun by intuition, developed in a heartfelt encounter, and came full circle with a surprise and anonymous gift.

Another of the now standard expectations that reward as well as undermine generosity is tax relief. In our society giving would likely decline precipitately if something were not given back, yet this is exactly the meaning of conditional generosity. There is nothing wrong with giving purely for a tax receipt, but in a sense this is only partially about generosity. So too is funding charitable functions, or donating to building funds, in the cause of getting sponsoring rights for individuals or companies. Acknowledgment is certainly a worthwhile reward for this kind of philanthropy, but there is a fine line between purchase and purpose. Without *mercy* or *compassion* at the source of such giving, the reciprocity of aggrandizement can make the generosity mean or secondary. Little *courage* and even less *humility* is expended when so much is expected and subsequently received back.

It is certainly not our intention to dismiss the contribution that commercialized charity makes. Good things do indeed happen from such gifts. The salient issue is not to mistake this for generosity. Even Live Aid concerts can be effective yet numbing when celebrities use their status to bring awareness and funds to a cause they have chosen to support. As entertainment audiences, we, in turn, give to the cause and receive the concert. The question becomes, what's next? What do we need to receive next time to be induced to give? Is the need not enough? Does poverty really need pop superstars to validate the dire need and cause our hearts to focus? Ticket holders do bond in their relationship with entertainers, sharing values for worthy causes. Everybody feels good, but does anyone or anything change? History shows not. Usually absent from the bond in spectacularly staged giving events are those in most need. The poor and hungry receive benefits but in some way the despair is even greater, and the gulf in relationship wider, when stellar intermediaries are needed to gain the attention that simple common decency really owes them. By being so exceptional, giving through concerts and special high-tech events tests the basic virtue of *reliability;* will our motivation to give still be there when the spotlight turns away?

In our culture, as in most others, giving takes on a form of ritual, reminding people of what matters, and to honour those close to them. However, too often the ritual has become little more than a mass sales event. Rushing around store-hopping, and experiencing stress and fatigue in the name of giving, turns generosity into a paradox. The generative relationship that true generosity promises cannot be experienced in such circumstances. Giving gifts, cards and flowers for birthdays, anniversaries and special occasions, such as Christmas, can easily fall into the category of conditional generosity. Many give because they have always given, or because it is expected of them, or they feel obligation to a person from whom they've received. There is nothing wrong in this customary reciprocity but what gets lost in the rote is to give because you *want* to show your love and respect for another. Love provokes us to be creative in giving, to ponder the needs of the other and to enter into a relationship with the recipient.

Most of us, at one time or another, have received strange gifts. These situations raise the question of how much we have been seen by the giver, and how much he or she has observed our needs, or even inquired about them. The strange gift usually reflects the desires of the giver rather than those of the recipient. Both of us have been culpable of passing on presents we disliked or didn't want, or rushing to buy any old gift on our way to an occasion. We, too, have been burdened by the responsibility of receiving gifts we know we will never use. We ponder the value of those circular newsletters—all about the family, and usually not our own. Invariably, there is little or no relationship in being sent facts about others' experiences, however extraordinary they may be. The point we are making is that we are filled only by the loving actions of others *particular* to ourselves.

On the other hand, we have been profoundly touched receiving simple surprises when we least expected them. We are moved by single acts of creativity—poems, prayers, handmade cards—that reflect the time and love of the giver who has acknowledged us in a special way. Hindsight has even led us to certain revelations regarding Christmas gift giving. A few years ago, we decided (as a couple and not unanimously as a family) to donate money to a charitable cause in lieu of material presents. We composed a card to explain the cause we were supporting and we sprinkled our envelopes under the tree, relieved that we hadn't had to spend hours with the wrapping paper and ribbon, and parcel tags.

Being so enwrapped in our do-goodness, we missed the disappointment on the faces of family members, especially the younger ones. We had done the right thing maybe, but not in a generous way, because we had imposed a perspective that withheld the joy and excitement that receiving a special gift can give. We were self-absorbed in our one-way giving, making it easy for ourselves, without taking into account what others would want. Wishing to distinguish Christmas, we instead flattened the fun, because, although worthy, we had missed the real encounter of relationship. It was, in the end, as it was for Schmidt, all about us and nobody else. Humbled, we now take time to ponder the needs of each member of our family, and each friend. We keep our gifts simple. We still give to the causes we wish to support, but with quiet focus on their own integrity and not our conditional piggy-backing on some other occasion or event. In hindsight, and with a bit of wisdom, we've seen that our Christmas gifts of the past could well have contributed to both the person *and* the cause—in the spirit and virtue of *balance*—instead of one at the sacrifice of the other.

THE EXTRA MILE

Generosity defies easy rationale because it has most impact when it is excessive. Like freedom, generosity is not a 50/50 proposition. It takes extra effort to generate equality, or to bring equal degrees of fairness to those who have least power or voice. Of course, excess in giving warms others and promotes hope. But surplus generosity can also threaten friendships and undermine possibilities if it creates stresses in status or reciprocity. Practising excessive generosity, therefore, is risky as it has its ups and downs. Monitoring motives and staying true to the three-stage circle of giving, receiving and circulating—including the ten virtues that create a pure generosity— aids discernment in practising the necessary "extra-mile" giving, or what we like to call "double-and" generosity.

The parable of the good Samaritan provides an ideal example of this kind of giving. A man travelling from Jerusalem to Jericho falls into the hands of robbers, who beat him and leave him near death. The few people who pass him by turn away. However, a Samaritan is moved by pity and compassion, bandages his wounds, and brings him to a local inn, where he pays the innkeeper to take care of the stranger. Later the Samaritan returns to pay the full bill for the man's stay. The predominant lesson is about kindness to strangers. But the significant feature is the effusiveness of generosity. The Samaritan's "double-and" is in attending not only to the emergency, but also to the recovery: shouldering the responsibility to help in crisis while also investing in the victim's long-term restoration to health and wholeness.

Once upon

AN OPEN WINDOW

An intercontinental family crisis. Stop. Woman organizing global conference in Italy has last-minute setback. Stop. Cook got sick. Stop. Participants from around the world already en route. Stop. Husband back in North America bemoans situation to sister. Stop. She says, "I'll go and help." Stop.

This is the sister who feared travelling alone. The eldest daughter of immigrants, she straddled two worlds; did double jobs, working and expected by her mother to take care of her much younger siblings. This was the sister whom the mother most leaned on. And that was the problem. For being always there, she was taken for granted. Mother was now dead. Years had passed. But the hurt lingered. Despite sacrifices and accomplishments, self-esteem seemed too tightly bound to others' appreciation. She missed Mother. And she missed being truly recognized by her.

Still, the generosity that defined her spirit could not be suppressed. That brother needed help was all she needed to know. Despite her foreboding about international flights, she booked herself on a plane for the next day. For a week she cooked, and scrubbed, and did the unseen duties, which made the conference a success. After all these years, she was once again sitting in for Mother. But somehow it felt different, especially in the country of their origin. She looked out the window while washing the dishes and in a flash saw her mother's face smiling at her. It may have been the golden light, or the lingering effects from jet lag. Maybe it was the endorphins from doing good, or just amazing grace. It didn't matter, because her heart was filled, perhaps for the first time, with Mother's love, and Mother's appreciation of her, and that was enough.

NB: "Going the extra mile" seems inconvenient, a literal dislocation. Yet if this is given from the heart, with risk to self, the rewards received can be life changing.

Generosity flourishes in going farther than expected. What is needed does not necessarily exhaust what is possible. With kindness, consideration and courtesy, giving takes on an element of not only surprise but also extraordinary hope in the capabilities of the human heart. Generous acts, however big or small, which include "double-and" graciousness, are contagious. When we read about, or witness, others' extraordinary generosity, we are moved to do something ourselves.

For instance, when one of us was ill for nearly a year, a friend delivered flowers she'd arranged herself every two weeks, bringing a bouquet of colour and fragrance that filled our house with her art. The spontaneous act—given not once but repeatedly with quiet consistency and constant love—brought us comfort and hope throughout the uncertainty of the long healing process. Other friends, a couple, hired a cook who was grateful for the work, to deliver boxes of prepared, three-course meals to our door. Beyond giving nourishment and comfort, it freed one of us from having to do dishes. Sometimes double-and giving means knowing that a person needs to receive again *and* again *and* again for the generative qualities to seed and sprout and grow. Caregivers do exactly this: giving carefully as the infirm have needs, and being so fully caring that the giving extends reliably throughout the days, months or years of the infirmity, without complaint.

This, in effect, shows the expansive and dynamic nature of generosity. In another of Jesus' teachings, he advises people to go the "extra mile." In the context of Jesus' time, the request to walk with someone was not an issue of

inconvenience. The need was the more basic
and precious one of safety. Walking together
provided protection. To go the "extra mile" is to
be moved beyond the terms of obligation and
into the realm of care, relationship and friendship. After doing what is needed—the first
mile—the second mile is simply for the mutual
and generative experience of togetherness.

One of the reasons many decline going the
"extra mile," especially in giving money, is the fear
of not having enough for one's own needs. We may
already "give at the office," or practise the ancient
art of tithing—giving away anywhere between 5
and 10 percent of our total income on a consistent
basis. Tithing is a valuable way of sharing what
abundance we receive with others. However, the
implication of the "extra mile" in tithing is that it
too is relational—it's not done for simply tax relief
or religious obligation but for the very real commitment to someone or something you care about
at your core. You care enough to show you do by
consistently giving, or you care enough to give
more than you feel comfortable parting with at a
time of having less. This is when generosity begins
to multiply its power—when you perhaps give

from not having enough, when you empty out your pockets and maybe even empty out your bank account, when you forget you can't afford to give, when you let go of the sense of ownership about money and goods. And the reason you do so is the exuberant rush and joy that come from helping others and forgetting yourself.

Once upon

A DREAM

She'd played the piano since she was a four-year-old. She loved tinkling the keys and learning new pieces. And she performed a few concerts when she was older. She'd always had a piano, an upright with a strong resonance, but she missed the sensitivity and bell-like song that a grand piano could give—like the one she had learned to play on as a child.

He was the first to recognize the pianist and artist in her. She played now only in the quiet of their shared home, nothing special, as there was little time to spare between the commitments of her job. He had the idea for her fiftieth birthday, still a few years away, but then, why should it wait? He wanted to honour her creativity with what was surely one of the best instruments in the world, a Steinway. Not being a piano expert, he asked her to go visit some piano dealers. She couldn't believe that he was doing this for her, and she struggled with accepting, and receiving, such an enormous gift. And the cost! He was so happy to be able to give that he emptied his bank account—all his money went in a flash on a solid black reconditioned 1920s Steinway.

What could she ever do to show her gratitude? The answer, he said, was to play it often. The old upright stood in the corner now. She knew a young woman who was saving for a piano on her limited salary. The old upright went straight over to her, with a note to remember to play it often.

NB: Gifts of magnitude go on giving for years and years and years. And these generate the opportunity to pass on gifts to another—to give, receive and circulate instruments of art, to support the expression of play, to fulfill the yearnings of creativity, to nourish and widen the heart to give on. The risks sometimes seem big, but so inevitably are the reverberations.

In the shamanic (native North American) tradition, there exists a unique ceremony of generosity called the giveaway, which unfolds as a transformational exercise of the heart. It is usually performed within a community—sometimes one to one—to honour and express sincere love of the other. The love is not so much in the giving of an object or objects that have emotional or material value to the giver, but in the power that is unleashed by that which is so dear. No one who partakes of a giveaway comes away emptyhanded. Everyone gives and receives and circulates. It is not an exercise in easy gift giving. It is, instead, a ritual of giving away something precious that hurts to give, that is difficult to part with. In a community or group, this ritual usually proceeds with each person laying his or her chosen giveaway object on an altar or central space to await its new owner. The relationship is not established at first. When everyone has parted with a gift, one by one each person goes forth to pick an object other than the one he or she set out. The order of selection is random, and each individual chooses what calls out as something he or she may need in the future. In this process people receive something precious to another, something given in love, and by receiving it step into tending the treasure for now. Mother Teresa taught that if you don't accept from another—however small the gift, however much you think they can't afford it, or shouldn't give a gift—you deny the joy of the giver. Givers experience joy when another receives what they have offered, especially the bittersweet joy of giving that which hurts to part with.

Once upon

A RING AND A RING OF BEADS

They were AA members on a retreat. They had travelled far together—emotionally, spiritually, mentally and physically. And they had been

sober for a long time. This weekend, they par-
took of a giveaway ceremony together. One of
them gave the only piece of family jewellery he
had, his dead father's ring. All the other family
valuables he had previously sold for drink. He
had hoped to give his own son this ring, he said,
as he pulled it off his finger and laid it on the
table. In the ensuing silence, a younger man
came forward and picked it up. He had been
unemployed for a while, and he and his wife had
been unsuccessfully trying for a child for over a
year. Not much had been going right for them.
He was not one to wear rings and things, but the
ring fit on his fifth finger, snugly, as if it had
always been meant to be there. That night he
and his wife conceived, and his dream of
becoming a father came true.

He was dying of cancer. Always a quiet man, he
was not one to express himself. His daughter
also had few words, but her feelings were of
overwhelming love and gratitude for him. As
she prepared to go and see him—possibly for

the last time—she looked around her house for an object to give him, something she couldn't part with that would express her loving feelings. She tried to ignore what was clearly calling her because she treasured those sacred meditation beads. She'd had them personally blessed by the Dalai Lama. She began to sob as she wrapped them in a silk pouch. She sobbed again handing them to her father. Dropping them into his outstretched, thin hand poking from the sheets, she began to cry. "It's the most I can give," she whispered.

"Then they are precious to me," he replied, "and I will keep them here near my heart," and he placed them in the chest pocket of his pajamas. "They are to help with a peaceful passing," she added. He met her eyes and smiled.

He died a few weeks later at his home, cared for by a company of visiting nurses. The nurse who came to lay him out and prepare his body for burial was a Buddhist. She carefully folded the *mala* beads through his clasped fingers, "for a peaceful passing," she said. The nurse stayed on with the family after the funeral, cooking and caring for them.

After she left, the family sent her flowers at the place she said she worked, a nursing hospital in the nearby town. But no one knew of her there. "Are you sure?" the wife asked. "We've never heard of her," was the reply. Whoever she was, and wherever she came from, they agreed they'd been visited by an angel.

NB: We may think we are owners, but we are only borrowers. We may believe we are giving, but we are only passing on. We may think we lose what we give, but we actually find much more. By giving that which we don't want to part with as an expression of love, honesty and vulnerability, we are humbled by what is revealed and healed. We contribute to the miraculous by giving what hurts. The evidence of the extraordinary is seen in everyday acts of "double-and" and "extra-mile" generosity.

THE TRAUMA OF TOO MUCH

Giving away what you value so much that it hurts to give it is a rare act of love. It is a test of intention and integrity—intention for the clarity about the nature of our attachment and the motive for our giving; integrity for whether it will heal. This is why *balance* is one of the most important if the least obvious virtues of generosity. There is a very real narrow line between balancing the upside of "extra-mile" and "double-and" generosity with the downside excesses of endless, self-exhausting generosity. Getting our giving right requires us to be aware of how much another can receive. If you have much to give, it is wise to be honest and discerning about your motives and in which area you will be giving the greater benefit.

Giving excessively can frequently fall into a form of bribe. An excessive giver's hidden message could be "Look how indispensable I am," or even less generously, "Look how much you owe me by how much I have given you." If the gift—or gifts—are not for, from and with love, and to satisfy the needs of the other, then something else is at play, usually a hidden transaction expecting reciprocity, or competition to earn status or special position. One December we viewed a television documentary in England on the excesses of Christmas gift giving in

Hollywood. Top celebrity agents had employed teams of gift buyers to find the perfect bag, or ornament, or whatever extravagant object they thought suitable for the stars they represented. The program showed them sorting through the items and price tags. The bigger the star's earnings, the more they felt compelled to spend. The program documented the excess of excesses as a news item. What was missing altogether was any relational exchange: the audience got no closer to the real humanity of the celebrities, and never saw whether the expensive and carefully chosen gifts were actually generative. Rather than expose another side to generosity, this info-news about extravagant giving was simply spectacle.

A subtler example of the underside of excessive giving is when the motivation or intent is unclear or distorted. One such case was when a young bachelor executive befriended a couple he had met on the job. They would go to dinner, movies and the theatre together on weekends. They would also give relatively expensive gifts to each other for birthdays and special events. One Christmas the executive bought airline tickets for the trio to go to New York. While they seemed to have a great time together, the slightly profligate trip tipped the balance in the friendship. There was something awkward about the scale of the gift that embarrassed both sides, and soon after, the couple ceased calling. The executive, initially hurt that what he thought was his generosity was unappreciated, later realized he had gone over the top in a last-minute rush. Perhaps this trip had been more about celebrating his success than about celebrating as friends, or the couple felt some shame for not keeping up with the gifts race. Whatever the reason, the expense did not compensate for the thoughtlessness. As a result, the symmetry of sharing and receiving and circulating had been broken. There is little *compassion* in grandiosity; there is little *mercy* in imposing an extravagant gift that is too much to receive. Without *humility,* the executive had disrespected the *balance* in generous giving, to the point, it turned out, of no return.

Generosity is not always about giving more. It is about loving more in the giving. And it is about being aware of the balance required between the needs of both giver *and* receiver.

GIVING

Once upon

⌒

A BOTTLE

She needed rest after a long year of caring for
her aging parents. The cabin she rented on a
river, at the end of a dirt track an hour from
town, was a primitive place with no plumbing,
but it was beautiful. She spent two weeks sleeping and then a friend back home e-mailed her.
She had a friend recovering from illness who
needed time away. Could this friend stay with
her for a week or two? Her first reaction was
one of anger at the intrusion into her newly
found isolation and rest, but after a day of discerning she said yes. It seemed wrong to deny
someone the peace she had received.

The time together proved to be nourishing
for them both; they had much in common,
including appreciating the outdoors and being
quiet. While her guest prepared to depart on a
bus to the train station, she offered her her last
bottle of water for the trip as there were no
stores nearby. She could drive into town tomorrow to buy more—she'd manage.

That night, alone again, she felt tired and wished she could stay in the cabin for a day or two more without having to get water for herself. In the morning, as she woke to the prospect of no coffee, she went to the kitchen to find, to her amazement, not a bare cupboard but another bottle of water.

NB: If you give out of your own emptiness for another's need, what replenishes you may come as a surprise.

Time Is More Precious Than Money

The prevalent complaint of not having enough time to do what one would wish—or dream about—or even to do what is asked—can change only with individual change. Earlier in this book we explored the generosity of change in attitude, life situations and action, along with the necessity of being generous to ourselves. Generosity to self usually involves, at bare minimum, giving time to oneself for rest, balance, contemplation and healing. Inclined to clichés—"Time is money," "Time doesn't wait," "Time flies" (as we run out of it)—we are also party to the commonest question, "Where did the time go?" (We hope that we won't be asking that same question at the end of our lives!) Much of the anxiety and relational breakdown in the examples about celebrity gifts and traumatic travel had to do with not having enough time to do the *discerning*. This is awareness—weaving the thread of what is desired and hoped for in the giving into the fabric of life, friends and fulfillment. Missing the process of discernment endangers the possibilities of making a difference. Discernment activates the intelligence in our hearts, enabling our generous acts to be honest and true.

Many heroes of generosity, such as Mahatma Gandhi and Mother Teresa, are people who have made a difference not only by their lives, but also by their teaching, attitude and philosophy. Sometimes the heroes and heroines of generosity are less famous, such as French Jewish philosopher Simone Weil, who, wishing to understand with her heart, tested her intellectual contribution to the rights of workers by taking on humble and dangerous jobs in heavy industry and on a fishing boat. These remarkable individuals have left us with a legacy from which to generate more generosity. They each discerned—through study, experiments of the heart and quiet reflection—where to concentrate their talents, and how to consistently offer what was most needed, including the gift of themselves.

Time is the most precious gift. Time can actually slow and expand if you know *where* you are to share it. You may know how much time to give or to whom you will give, but you also have to know *where* you are to practise your giving to be in the necessary *balance* of generosity. When you know where you are to give, then you will find that time doesn't have such a stranglehold upon your life; time can be on your side. In discovering *where* you can give, you may have to move on from fair-weather friends, or people who drain your energy, to those who can offer a community of similar intention, putting love into action. As it is impossible to give time to everybody who asks it of you, it is advisable to make room—and space—in your life to consciously practise giving in the right ways, and in the right places. This is the wisdom of *balance* and *discernment.*

Giving time, as an art of right living, actually requires more *discernment* than giving money. When time is given, it is not just an hour or two, or an evening at a soup kitchen, or a chat on the phone; generous people offer their hearts and their gifts to regenerate others. Nevertheless, juggling project after project of diverse giving, with personal energy spread out or dispersed all around us, will eventually tire and paralyze a person into the all-too-common state of giving what is left over, while feeling there is nothing left to give. This, sadly, is another trauma—the trauma of too much time given away, and not enough time given to discerning the two-way flow of *mercy, compassion, humility, hope and trust.*

This sort of endless—and persistent—giving is bound to lead to burnout. Burnout is especially common in women, many of whom are inclined to deny themselves in trying to do it all. In their persistence on giving, as well as fixing, others' lives, they rush around doing as much good as possible. Giving to as many as need them, they end up stifling what is self-generative, because they have denied any particular act of love the time to be fully expressed. They say, "Here I am, giving you what you need, but I can't stay a minute, as I'm needed somewhere else." These sorts of experiences are potentially more harmful for the recipient than receiving nothing at all, since what often gets passed on is some of their guilt. If people concentrate on *where* they will practise their giving, then they can give much more in the quality of generosity than just a quantity of fix-me-ups. In generous giving of your time, you are not in competition with another— and not in competition with yourself to do as much as you would like or want. You need to have time to give time. You need to give what is genuinely needed, not to give what is left over. And you need to have the *courage* to do less to enable you to have the *balance* to give more.

The Best Medicine—Give What You Need to Receive

This lesson was inspired by a friend who learned its wisdom by living it. As a single mother with an infant at home, she had hardly any income, was tired and worried about the future, and generally felt sorry for herself. It was winter, the nights were long, and she fell further into depression. She realized, at some point, that no one was going to help her but herself, so she made the difficult leap of faith to give what she needed to receive—companionship, care and time to other women isolated in their homes with scarce support. This was the beginning of her extraordinary and consistent generosity, where, through her practice of "giving what she needed to receive," she has literally helped hundreds of people. And she received everything she needed herself by giving to others. She continues practising this today by helping those who are sick—even dying—to continue to give what they need, and to remember others' suffering in their own suffering. She has organized women in nursing homes to knit scarves for children in Afghanistan; she has connected housebound women to cook meals for those who can't prepare their own food; and she helps women on the street by including them in creative acts for the community.

Giving what you need to receive can be in small acts of love to not only others but also yourself. It is a precious principle of giving that can be practised by anyone. And it moves one from a passive helplessness—even victimization—to an active generative way of not only living but also giving.

Once upon

~

A LOST SOUL

He had been diagnosed with schizophrenia, which curtailed his ability to hold a regular job. He still lived with his parents, which made him feel helpless and inadequate. Although talented (a few of his poems had been published) and keen on helping people, he was unable to find his place in the world and had to be admitted to a hospital to overcome his depression.

While there he befriended an older man, much sicker than he. After a week or two he made the man laugh. He found that he could lift him from his despair and find the funny in the everyday. A few months later they both found an apartment together and became happy room-mates. Life turned for the better for both of them.

NB: Sometimes having the circumstances to share oneself leads to healing for another.

~

GIVING OURSELVES

When we are present to one another from the per-spective and practice of generosity, we become catalysts for each other's potential, infusing our environment with the generous capacities to help elevate people around us. If we are to be catalytic, then we have to be honest and truthful in sharing ourselves. If shyness or busyness is used as an excuse not to share ourselves, then we deny this generosity. By withholding expression of the gifts and talents we have received, or skills we have honed, we are not givers but withholders. We can-not be generous givers by being absent from involvement. We cannot be givers by being fearful of consequences or change. We cannot be givers if we worry about how much time it will take.

Parenting is one of those activities that requires constant and consistent giving of self to children. As well it is a regular exercise in forgetting oneself for the purposes of another, for their formation, happiness, security and growth. Parents are not only caregivers in the everyday, but also inspire hope and guidance for future lives.

Sharing yourself by giving what you have been given, offering what is needed, and risking to extend to others what you yourself ache to receive, draws you into the three-part circular movement of generosity. With steadfast steps in giving, you're on the path to that magnanimous incentive, receiving.

FIVE

Receiving

WE have co-dedicated this book to a man who inspired its themes and exemplified generosity in all its aspects, but especially in the art of receiving. As a husband, father, artist and musician, Lewis Vardey gave much to many. Yet his greatest art was to savour. A lover of jazz, Lewis taught family and friends to receive the off-tempo pulse of swing. He treasured every note. For him every improvisation was an invitation into the joy and surprise of what the Duke,

Count or Louis was offering. Lewis was rich in hearing what most of us miss, in receiving what the mysterious silence between notes reveals. And the way he listened and received, with such relish and enthusiasm, was irresistible to everyone who knew him, so that they couldn't help but join him tapping along.

Lewis made music—and fused his playing of the piano, guitar and saxophone on reel-to-reel and cassette tapes. He gave much because, although from a working-class background, he had received much. Lewis made his living as a commercial designer. One of his specialties—honed while freelancing for *Reader's Digest* predominantly as a book designer—was to shrink large advertisements, prepared by client agencies, to fit the smaller-than-normal magazine format. The art here was not simply to reduce, but to extract the essence of the creative idea, to magnify the message within the reduced frame. It took *humility* to work with other people's ideas, and *courage* to cut, paste and position the elements that preserved the integrity of the concept. Yet Lewis's work demonstrated how sensitively and respectfully he received the insight, the point of view and artistry

of others. As with jazz, Lewis practised his pro-
fession with a generous improvisation—receiving
the bass, adding tempo, feeling the drumbeat,
flashing his horn. He received everything that life
threw at him with an optimistic disposition, seeing
the humour in many of life's absurdities, and feeling it his duty to pass on what made him smile.

People long to share themselves and their creativity. "Give me the ability," goes the anonymous
seventeenth-century prayer, "to see things in
unexpected places and talents in unexpected people." We need collaboration with others to do this;
not only giving ourselves, but receiving the gifts
of others in our communities, families and workplaces. Whatever the aims or objectives, outcomes
and group goodwill depend on some catalytic,
constructive and creative mix of giving our personal best while receiving the best of others. At
work many individuals are pressed to function in
teams. Most of us know the disappointment or
alienation we feel when what we offer others—be
it time, attention, creativity or ideas—is ignored
or dismissed. What is generous and feels generative is to have our contribution seen, heard and
welcomed. We are enhanced when others receive

us. And we become trusted when we too are open and receptive to others.

Lewis's love of art, and freelance job as art director for *Reader's Digest,* qualified him as a critic. He recognized what worked and what did not. Being an artist, Lewis first respected the dignity of the effort. He understood the fragility of any creative concept, and considered it his job to showcase the creativity of others. Rather than criticize, his bias was to appreciate the hidden strengths in unexpected places. Instead of putting down what might not be the best, he tried to tweak concepts to emphasize the core of the initial inspiration. His work with others' art and creativity influenced our own thinking about the role and possibilities of a critique. Honesty is vital in order to see what's there and what's not. So too is evaluative judgment, in order to place a creative effort in its context, and to constructively engage the promise of its art. Yet, as Lewis showed, the quality of the critique depends on how much we are willing to receive. Too often criticism is practised solely as an exercise in giving: giving a thumbs-up or thumbs-down, giving a response that displays the critic's own cleverness, giving some aesthetic seal of approval that compliments the critic's own taste. Without receptivity, such a critique becomes a bludgeon. One author we know found herself attacked in a ruthless way by a critic in a national magazine. Her publishers—and other reviewers—could not find reasons for the venom. It turned out that the critic had been planning his own book on the same theme but intended to explore it from a different aspect. He later admitted that his prejudice had clouded his review. In effect, he was unable to receive what the original book had to offer because he was pre-empted in what he wanted to give.

Like all of us, Lewis had his faults and eccentricities. Having grown up on the harsh streets of London (his father had lived a stone's throw from Ye Olde Curiosity Shop Charles Dickens immortalized), Lewis could be obsessively suspicious. He constructed elaborate homemade security systems. While visiting Manhattan, he carried a second wallet filled with fake credit cards and xeroxed cash, to offer up to a potential thief. His home was never burgled and he was never robbed, so the irony for this man of extraordinary generosity was his all-too-human worry that what he had earned would be taken away from him. Being generous does not make us perfect but, as with Lewis, it inspires, transforms and resonates far beyond the limitations of our mortality or our imperfections.

Of his many skills, Lewis excelled as a water-colourist. He painted hundreds of landscapes in various parts of the world. Some are remarkably beautiful. Many are deeply evocative in the way they conceal detail in shadow or light. The art, beyond critical worth or commercial value, is what Lewis received and recorded with his brushes. Looking at a forest on the horizon, he always instructed his children to look carefully, to see that what was supposed to be green wasn't green at all, but black. He felt that a tree bare in winter was more exquisite than when fully in leaf in summer. As in other forms of artistic expression, whether painting, music, film, theatre, dance, literature or architecture, the generosity of the creator is evident in *how* we receive what has been given. When so alert to receive, we can see anew and appreciate more, and take far less for granted.

Lewis taught that all creativity should be an exercise in generosity. When moved by music, challenged by a painting, engrossed in a play or movie, we are, in effect, receiving the generosity of artists. Their vision touches us; their pathos evokes our own catharsis; their craft inspires our appreciation; their questions challenge our own answers. There is a flow between giver and receiver, a communication beyond words. While the aesthetic process hinges on give-and-take, there is no certainty or fixed return to the artist's gift. We all bring our own experiences and assumptions to an encounter with art. From this unique perspective we communicate in our own way *with* the art, and receive what we need.

As not all art or expression is generous, careful *discernment* is necessary in order to choose *what* to receive. Much of today's entertainment is conceived not to enliven but to numb. Escapism certainly releases stress, but in the same way that a pin releases air from a balloon; it encourages our passivity and leaves us nothing to receive. There is a definite distinction between what we receive and what we consume. Engaging art moves and transforms us. Consuming entertainment provides a short-term thrill with no lingering impression or consequence. Receiving artfully involves regeneration.

Some questions to ponder are, when have you been touched by art? When have you received any art that pulled you away from yourself into some wider experiences of truth? Listening to music, with our hearts as well as our ears, often helps us to truly listen to one another. Immersing ourselves in a painting or play helps us perceive something new, which is to receive something extraordinary. These virtues for receiving art correspond closely to those for being generous. For example, we need *courage* to expose our assumptions or prejudices to the quandaries posed by artists, especially to engage with what we may not like or easily understand, yet need to hear or see. We also need *humility* to silence our cares, concerns or presumptions to encounter the experience or interpretation or challenge offered by the art.

As with any generosity, we need *discernment* to sift through the dross, choosing what we personally need to receive to unleash our own creativity.

We need *hope* to give appropriate time and contemplation to what we receive, to allow awe or wonder, or distress, to unsettle what deadens us, and spark a renewal.

Receiving, as an aesthetic experience, requires the *mercy* to recognize the risk and the humanity of the artist.

As a stirring up of creative potential, receiving involves *compassion* for passion, for having our hearts inflamed with feelings and intuitions by the art we apprehend. There are no standards or predictable responses. With beauty, creativity or awe, we are engaging with mysteries of meaning. Compassion relishes excellence, not as final outcome but as the continuous opening to what is still to be seen, understood or learned.

Just as artists usually master craft skills with care and discipline, receiving is based on some aspect of constancy or *reliability*. Such attentiveness involves the skill of recognizing connective patterns, reading forms and symbols, appreciating continuities with history or tradition, as well as applauding risks. In practising receiving as an artist (which all of us are—artistic expression is not reserved for a few), we need to ask ourselves questions—for example, "What fills you up?" "What inspires your imagination?" "When have you felt awe?"

As writers, we have had some of these satisfactions in creating books and serving readers, but this generative activity seems to us to always be an overflow from what we have received from other writers. St. Augustine wrote, "Receive what you are and be what you receive." This advice is an invitation to always stand on "the shoulders of giants" (Isaac Newton) who have shaped our consciousness and our forms of expression. Artists understandably tend to focus more on their burdens, disappointments and distractions, yet within society or at work, in leisure or productivity, and even in prayer, we are all standing on high mountains of receiving. Before we add our bit, it is good to remember that we are enabled, empowered and enhanced by all the ideas, stimulus and understanding proffered to us. We may choose not to share generously, but none of us can realistically exempt ourselves from receiving the generosity that has been thrust upon us as living, thinking, feeling, creative and free human beings.

The virtue of *remembering* strengthens us in generosity for the future. Tomorrow is a promise all expect to receive. To acknowledge what has been received, to honour the worth and appreciate the potential, requires us to reflect on what has moved us in the past and contemplate how we can bring forth from ourselves to create beauty or originality or heroic action.

It takes time to receive with consciousness and gratitude, and it takes time to work through implications. Receiving is itself a creative act. This is counterintuitive for many of us because the idea of receiving seems to imply some personal lacking, or failure in self-sufficiency. The truth is that we curtail generosity when we curtail receiving. We not only deny the worth of what is offered and deprive givers of their due and their joy, but also debase our own worthiness as creative agents, catalysts and artists.

Once upon

~

A MUM

The quandary was not unusual. She was distressed nevertheless. Her teenage son with a good heart and gentle artistry was being bullied. Losing weight as quickly as confidence, the young man was in a downward spiral of stress.

Mum spoke softly on the phone to her brother. Such discussions were not unusual because theirs was a close family. But something had shifted in that the details were now more intimate and the worries more raw. Counsel and questions passed back and forth. Over several conversations Mum allowed herself to receive another perspective, other suggestions, and the consolation of being heard. It felt better to have shared for the good of her son.

In time—quick time, this being the "teen age"—the crisis passed. What lingered was the appreciation. Mum had been in need and had reached out. She had allowed her brother's advice to help her be a good mother. But the real generosity was in the receiving on both sides: Mum received being heard by her brother, and the brother received her concern and vulnerability.

NB: Our greatest giving can often be our willingness to receive, which creates an opening for truth to be shared and for love to grow.

THE SPIRIT IN RECEIVING

Receiving is a moral quality as well as an artistic endeavour. Our basic human rights are not so much entitlements as received through the responsibilities upheld by others. Thus, what we owe one another is intertwined with what we hope to achieve. Our choices should be inspired and tested by what we, ourselves, ought to receive. A good corollary to the golden rule is to receive from others as we would hope to be received—receiving their gifts, ideas, perspective, even if different or challenging to us, as we would hope to have our best efforts received by them. The reciprocity involved is not only between people but also within each individual. Without relishing what you've already received you are inclined to be continually dissatisfied, only wanting more. A healthy *balance* is required between being a conscious, appreciative receiver and an imaginative, reliable giver. If you have the luxury of abundance, you need to be clear about how much to give, where and when. If you are in need of others' generosity, you need to be clear about how much to receive. This balance is not automatic because life's exigencies are never neat, fairly dispersed or in perfect proportion. Nonetheless, your own generous aim is to monitor your experience of generosity to achieve some artful balance between receiving and giving.

From our experiences growing up in religious households, we have seen how religions, when they become too dogmatic, miss this balance. "'Tis better to give than receive" goes the adage. Sometimes, however, this commendable altruism crosses the line. "Giving up" bad habits, temptations and wrongdoing are made part of a strict continuum that includes "giving" to others. Charity so prescribed becomes ascetic—to give at all costs, and give up desires and attachments, including any relishing of material abundance. Rigid overemphasis on giving and giving up has, in many cases, distorted the generous spirit at the heart of most religions. It has also bred, particularly among Christians, a personal inability to receive. It is simply much easier to keep on giving, and avoid the guilt of receiving, by ensuring the door is always closed to such possibilities.

Obviously, not all religious teachings are so anemic. Much of what is captivating about religions is the sense of purpose or meaning, including that derived from doing good works or contributing to the welfare of others. Mystics teach that spiritual growth happens when we receive that which is difficult for us to receive. If we are pronounced and active givers it is wise to consider the possibility that generosity also springs from a foundation of what has been received. American theologian and writer John Haughey calls this state "receivement." In Haughey's view, the love and friendship of God are already ours to be accepted. Instead of continually carrying the burden of trying to make a difference, every person already possesses what confers dignity and worth. When there is faith in God, it is natural for the relationship with the Divine to be based to some degree on receiving God's guidance, on conforming to God's will before giving anything, particularly what it is we'd like to give. One woman we know, who has done considerable work in helping communities around the world build housing and improve public health, always prays at a shrine near her home before she goes into action. She believes that she cannot receive the guidance and energy to do what she

needs to do without this spiritual discernment—
without receiving the grace and strength to carry
out her calling to help others.

Another woman, now in her eighties, has lived
with much suffering yet has always been a generous
giver. Her benevolence became part of her identity.
Once she had become unable to keep giving
because of her physical incapacities, she not only
found it hard to receive, but also felt a sense of
worthlessness. Through prayer her lamenting subsequently shifted to gratitude, and she has come to
realize quiet, peace and tranquility as rewards for a
full life, and a life full of giving.

Facing the test of receiving is referred to in
various religious traditions. In Buddhism, the
human mind stills and sheds illusions of ego and
coveting to receive *darshan* (grace) in its flow. In
many of his stories Jesus spoke of waiting, being
alert and prepared to welcome the blessings coming towards us. There is always a gift ready and
waiting to be bestowed. To receive, the soul must
do the work of becoming empty—unlearning
what clutters, unwinding what stresses and undo-
ing what exhausts. In modern society waiting is
usually a frustration, an inconvenience that

wastes time. But for spiritual seekers, the waiting is a heightened state of productivity for making space for truth and love. Accepting love, and receiving acceptance for the person we are, fulfills some of our most intense desires. Opening to the possibilities of "receivement" requires a letting go of control, an emptying of agendas, a dismantling of busy lives and a calming from distraction. This process, in spiritual terms, always begins within. If in stillness you can meditate on the love and generosity around you, you will begin to experience what this receivement *feels* like. If you can spend some time familiarizing yourself with doing nothing, resting without being restless, then you allow a state of being to be born within you, one that is glorious and free. And this state will be accompanied by remarkable synchronicities and miracles that drop in your path, ones you would never have recognized or imagined possible when insisting on control.

This path towards being more open to receive is not an easy one to take. We lead complicated lives, full of far too much information, and far too many daily experiences that do not nourish us but just add stress to our already stressful existence.

The hard realization is that we are the only ones responsible for the way our lives are—no one but ourselves can be blamed—and therefore we are responsible for changing them for the better. If you desire change and do not direct that change, then it is not inconceivable that you will be made ill by your intransigence. In most cases, illness and suffering allow us to ask for, and receive, help and therefore become experienced in receivement. When we suffer we cannot do anything but receive medical help, slow down and listen to the wisdom in our bodies; we cannot do anything but allow others to take care of us, advise us, sit with us, bring us food, say prayers for us, talk at depth with us. All frivolities are pushed aside, masks are removed and truth is revealed in the necessary receiving.

Once upon

A RUNAROUND

She had been a giver all her life and loved to please others. She would even end her conversations with friends and colleagues with the phrase "If you need anything you can rely on me." So everyone did rely on her, so much so that she hardly had a minute to herself. That changed when she fell and broke her leg. Unable to leave her house with a heavy plaster cast, she was forced to slow down. She hadn't experienced being in need. This made her suffer more than the pain in her leg. She tried to carry on for herself but it was impossible.

She had to receive. And more than this, she had to ask for help because most who knew her thought that she was all right, she'd manage as she always did. She was confronted with the truth that her running around to please everyone was a front for her own inadequacies. And now that she was vulnerable and not able to care for herself, she broke down and asked.

A close friend cooked and cleaned for her, and another helped her bathe, and both said how much it empowered them to give something to her. She realized then that she had denied others any chance of compassion towards her because, in her enthusiasm, she had run them into a tight and hopeless corner.

When she could walk without her crutches she decided that a balance between giving and receiving was necessary, for her future health and for those around her.

NB: It is imperative to make space to receive as well as give in order to balance generosity's delicate scales.

We have met people who believe that they are somehow unworthy of receiving what they really need. We have met others convinced that receiving the windfall of a large lottery will allow them to finally live out their desires, and then be generous to others. And we have talked to many people our age (mid-fifties) who plan to do what they really have wanted to do all along only when they retire. It is depressing to consider how much personal worth is bound up in money. Unable or too busy to relish what we have, unwilling to change even for what we know matters most, we experience a type of misery from miserliness. We are miserly towards ourselves when we do not take full vacations, or weekly Sabbath, or early retirement. We are miserly when we do not reward ourselves for a lifetime of work by taking a sabbatical, or changing what makes our lives unhealthy. We are miserly towards ourselves in ignoring our inner lives, our creativity and spirituality, in favour of further material gain, or to feed our fear of not having enough, and always wanting more. We are miserly towards ourselves in taking our own gifts for granted, or ignoring them, or putting them on hold, so we can make the money we want doing something else. And we are miserly towards our own receiving because we can feel guilty for having a desire that needs meeting.

This is especially pronounced among women, who primarily take on the responsibilities of givers, minders, protectors, organizers, lovers, cleaners, shoppers, drivers, officer managers, workers, caretakers and volunteers, with no idea of what it is they need to receive. The common excuse is "There's not enough time." The underlying fallacy is "I can't receive because of all the giving I'm doing." The truth is that time is ours to do with as we wish. Paradoxically, time stretches

and elongates according to the amount of emptiness we make available for ourselves. As hard as
we may try, we cannot resolve being too busy by
trying to do something about it. Take care with
priorities. Be *reliable* towards yourself, setting
boundaries, staying true to what is most important. And be rigorous cutting out unnecessary
information: regulate your availability to e-mail
and cellphones, curtail news consumption to what
matters; and find ten minutes a day for personal
reflection on what you need. This is why "Less is
more" is a central spiritual principle—a teaching
that only in practice reveals its secrets, surprises
and opportunities. We cannot receive when we are
full, but the emptier we are, the more we are free
to receive.

Generosity, however, cannot live if we *only*
receive. Nor can it exist without a foundation in
receiving. As essentially social beings, we
become givers from first being recipients; we
become experts from first being students; we
become artists or business people from first
being apprentices or trainees; we become parents after first being children; we become whole
spiritually after receiving grace and entering

into relationship with the transcendent. And, in many cases, the most generous thing we can give to one another is to simply receive.

Once upon

~

A COIN

She was famous for her work with the poor in the streets of Calcutta. One day a beggar by the road ran up to her with a small coin—financially worthless to anyone but him. It was his day's take, after a long, hot and humid toil, and he wanted to give it to her. She pondered what to do. If she took the money then he would have nothing at all, but if she rejected him, it would perhaps hurt him by insulting his spontaneous generosity. She stretched out her hand—he, who never had the chance to give, could give to Mother Teresa. The joy on his face said everything to her.

NB: Saying no to another's offer denies that person the joy of giving. Accepting what someone wishes to

give—even if you don't need it—allows the other's
heart's expression, and provides for renewed dignity.

~

RECEIVING MOMENTS

One of the most effective exercises in gaining
wisdom in receiving what you need is to take a
day to yourself (no phone, no distractions, completely alone). Lie on the floor with arms outstretched; take slow, long breaths; allow your
thoughts to be focused only on your breath as
you travel down from your mind's eye to the
deepest, darkest depths of your body. As you
become familiar with this place, you can ask
yourself the following questions—and the small
voice within, which holds your greatest wisdom,
will answer truthfully.

1. What do I need?
2. How can I receive it?
3. What can I do to make this happen?
4. Who can also help me?

What You Need Needs You

One day, already feeling a call to make some changes in her life, a businesswoman visiting a friend noticed a calendar of quotes on her desk. She was drawn to the one that stated, "What you need needs you." (It felt like a mantra to her as she repeated it to herself.) After considering what she most needed, she put an end to her isolated existence and reached out to her local community by volunteering. Although she had a full week of other obligations, her most fulfilling time was at the soup kitchen, being with people she'd never had a chance to encounter. And it was there that she met a fellow volunteer with whom she developed a relationship, and with whom she then initiated other projects in the community.

Personal needs and desires are separate neither from the greater whole nor from each other. As explained earlier, generosity lives beyond one's self, effecting creative change in the world while also changing each individual. "What you need needs you" exemplifies the symbiotic possibility of a more complete, life-giving, life-enriching future. When our desires are realistic—and not stuck in fantasies like winning the lottery—we then meet the larger energy for us to regenerate, recreate, restore the peace that is awaiting us all from one single act of generosity: one changed life.

This is another lesson we drew from the creative generosity of Lewis, in this case from the artful way in which he died. Succumbing after a long struggle with cancer, Lewis was at home with his family for the final weeks of his life. All five adult children were also back home, or near home. With careful—and invisible—planning by his wife, Edwina, Lewis gave himself over to each family member, asking and receiving what only they, as creative individuals, could give him. One gave a foot massage. Another prepared and fed him his favourite fruit. The one most proficient with her hands was asked to construct a wooden pedestal to support his feet. The one who had difficulty expressing feelings was allowed to sit with him in silence. And the one most gifted in telling stories was left to talk Lewis through the pathway of one of his watercolour paintings, a flower-filled wood in spring that recalled some of his greatest joys, as he took his final breath. Brief moments of receptive attentiveness towards each child allowed each one to give their father something that was distinctly and preciously theirs. He received, we realized only much later, what each needed to give. And in the process, he helped the family's grief by allowing each to be active in his dying, to give as he received, which began the healing of his passing before he had gone.

A genius of generosity, Lewis showed us that receiving can sometimes be the most profound and life-altering form of giving. And, in his inimitable style, he made sure that the woman he loved—and was married to for forty-six years—would still be reminded of his love through creative surprises. Writing love letters over many years that he hid in sealed envelopes in files and drawers, he ensured that they could be found when it was time for them to be discovered—in most cases, after he died. We marvel at the generosity, ingenuity, thoughtfulness and love that composing those letters took. He was a man who provided for his family; who, with his wife, took in his mother-in-law to live with them; who commuted to the city every day of the week to earn a living and still painted, sculpted, taught and expressed himself in his spare time. This spare time yielded the fruits of his generosity. It is what he did in his spare time that now generates our fondest memories, our family's enriching treasures.

Life is a gift received. Learning and growing happen from receiving teachings and receiving care. To belong is to be received. To love, in its fulfillment, involves receiving the beloved, while being so received by the other. To forgive allows us to receive another's contrition for mistakes and errors so that the other can be received as human. Much of what it means to be human pivots on receevement. This receiving entwines us in the needs and capacities of generosity, which enables circulation.

SIX

Circulating

To BE generative is to have lasting influence. Circulating occurs when what has been given and received ripples out into a larger environment. The movement beyond giving and receiving cannot be easily predicted or programmed. And sometimes the generosity is in receiving what seems unacceptable, or giving what is unimaginable, such as generating hope from calamity, or help from suffering. Circulating spreads when we dare to share, for the greater good, what we've experienced.

At a peace conference in Vienna, we had the privilege of meeting Irish Nobel laureate Mairead Corrigan Maguire. She had just addressed the delegates without notes, and then shared with us lessons about living within one's truth, and acting outwardly in one's love. Corrigan Maguire, along with Betty Williams, won the Nobel Prize in 1976 for organizing a series of peace marches in Northern Ireland after three children of Corrigan Maguire's sister, Anne, were killed by a gunman's getaway car. Tens of thousands turned out, with Catholics and Protestants marching alongside. The peace was a long time in coming. Nonetheless, through what seemed like an astonishingly foolish act— responding to violence with outstretched and forgiving hands—they broke the cycle of never-ending acrimony. Suddenly humanity and hope were introduced into a landscape of darkness and grief. Corrigan Maguire, Williams and their journalist friend Ciaran McKeown denied violence the final say by sharing their personal grief. They took it upon themselves to be generous instead. Doing so, they sowed generative seeds for broken families, divided communities and a war-weary world. Whether refusing to receive what perpetuates despair, or giving an offering that goes beyond the immediate horizon of what seems realistic, the example from Corrigan Maguire is that generosity can be, in a single act, practical, aspirational and healing.

Circulating is not enclosed within giver and receiver. Nor is it giving back in equalizing measure what has been received, which is the more usual impulse: "I have received this, therefore I must be worthy of it by giving something back to the giver." Instead, circulating is standing in the opportunities of either giving or receiving in ways that pass on the generosity of one to many. As an art of the heart, circulating involves the giver in an enabling for the receiver, which realizes its promise beyond either of them. Both parties in a generous encounter share what are the first of many waves that ripple out and touch others. Not every generous act must or will lead to a brave new social outcome. Yet, as a creative force, the impact of generosity works as a whole that is greater than the sum of its parts. This is why circulating (as the overarching part of the circular process of giving and receiving) is enlivened only in community. It is by definition impossible to practise circulating in isolation. Circulating can begin to live, and thrive, only when it has a community in which to be effective and able to grow.

As happened with Corrigan Maguire, generosity, in circulating, is about sharing oneself with others in a manner that creates, expresses or renews community. So great is the current social focus on the individual, and on the importance of self-interest, that the larger sense or appreciation of community has diminished or even perished. In truth, none of us can exist without each other: no one can thrive—or practise generosity— without the civil engagement that Plato described as "the family of families." Communities are usually founded on common principles and beliefs, with shared memories, priorities, intentions and mission. A generous community is one that is ordered and inspired by the human needs of all its members. More precisely, a generous community is defined by its priority for the poor.

Poverty tends to be demarcated by statistics about levels of income or unemployment. Certainly there is now, again, a pressing need to creatively address the underlying structural problems and imbalance that stunt participation or corrupt the human experience of so many members of the community. In addition to scoping out what society should give in terms of relief or infrastructure, we also need to honestly examine forces or factors that are chronically ungenerative—which actually reverse generosity by sustaining a degeneration of hope, opportunity or belonging. Poverty, as even many of us who are not poor can attest, can be a deficit far more onerous than lack of money. There is the poverty of enthusiasm caused by injury or ill health; the poverty of fellowship experienced by a troubled or uneasy mind; the poverty of missing joy through a hurt or closed heart; the poverty of being without meaning; as well as the poverty of generosity resulting from not having experienced the blessings and expansive potential of giving, receiving or circulating, somewhere, sometime, on this planet. Impoverishment on any of these levels produces the vacuum that keeps hope and regeneration stuck without expression. If generosity is expressed in circulation, poverty opposes it by separating and isolating needs and emotions, regardless of income or social status.

Our experience in circulating has shown us that communities of generosity sometimes spring up in a moment, spontaneously, as people are called to address these various forms of poverty. These communities are frequently informal, seeded by a mutual concern, a binding of purpose and compassion. In the face of tragedy, people come together to raise funds, offer consolation, or find some way to share grief and raise hope out of despair. Other times communities are founded by a visionary leader, whose intent and example inspire others to join and contribute. Movements for the emancipation of slaves, for women's right to vote, for collective bargaining of workers, for civil rights, and to oppose apartheid in South Africa fomented communities of interest whose aim in some way addressed imbalance, challenged structural poverty, and unleashed new potential for dignity, involvement and equality.

One poignant example of a generous community premised on circulation is the one founded by French Canadian Jean Vanier. The L'Arche community was begun in 1964 when Vanier opened the doors of his home—a bucolic house in the countryside of Trosly, France—to three men with disabilities. His intention was to offer an alternative to institutional life by having people with mental and physical challenges live as a family in a loving environment. His motive was to receive people as important and vital as they are, and not the way society would wish them to be. Jean Vanier began his circulating with a group of three, establishing that relationships are at the heart of community. Now there are over 120 L'Arche communities, based on the original model, all around the world.

Communities of generosity either implicitly or explicitly believe, and practise, the virtues of generosity—deriving *courage* from being a group; practising *discernment* as a debate and dialogue; having the *humility* to listen, co-operate and support one another; enabling the collective *compassion* to reach out beyond the joint interest of the group; showing *mercy* to those not yet belonging or treated fairly; practising with each other what they preach to others as proof of their *reliability;* managing *trust, hope* and *remembering* as exercises in renewing community; and *balancing* the needs and contributions of individuals with the aims and hopes of the totality.

History and social science research show that achieving radical, constructive change in situations of injustice depends upon the formation and cross-supports of community. While we all have responsibility for our rights and duties, the ethical sense that sustains fairness, balance and justice hinges on the understanding we derive from our conversations and collective experiences. Ethics is a plural and moral choice. For example, the *courage* to stand on principle often requires that one uphold the insights and principles of the community, reaching for not only what is necessary but also what the collective wisdom deems to be right. Perhaps the most powerful example of this interdependence in ethical courage and moral conduct comes from Martin Gilbert's unique study of the Holocaust. One of the world's foremost historians, Gilbert brought his scholarly investigation to bear in his book *The Righteous*. While most were silent in the face of the deportation of Jews, homosexuals and people with disabilities to death camps, a tiny minority of individuals—"the righteous"—risked their lives to help save those identified for extermination. Many thousands of people were saved. While they were but a fraction of those who perished, Gilbert wanted to expose the stories of those who so bravely went against the majority.

These people practised the highest form of generosity. They often risked denunciation and opprobrium from their own families and friends to follow their consciences. Sometimes a brave, solitary individual alone saved a person—or group—from capture and death. More often, though, Gilbert's research proved that it took one small community of eight to ten people, who came together to share resources, intelligence and concealments, to hide, feed and transport an otherwise doomed person to freedom. During the most repressive phase of the Nazi persecution, Gilbert found that it would take as many as fifty people to secure the life and liberation of a single person. To be "righteous" is always a personal choice involving personal risks, yet its purpose and fulfillment is almost always collaborative, enabling and finding completion through the bonds and aspirations of community.

Some people we know have found the "eight to one" ratio very motivating, as it removes what can be a burden of obligation and isolation from an individual confronting a need and wanting to help. However, many who are called to generosity, even when aware of this collective aspect of circulating, have a fear of committing to a community of any kind. This fear is usually based upon some imaginary scenario that requires a set of rules that a person is unable to follow, or an invisible hook that catches one for a longer-term commitment that is imagined as too onerous to sustain. This fear of commitment is all too common, which is why many phone in their generosity rather than personally connecting to people through giving, receiving and circulating. Instead of discerning together what is needed or what is right, instead of sharing together to define the priorities of the heart, many resort to occasional hands-on giving of money with a perceived no-ties freedom. This *ad hoc* giving is not truly circulating, if neither a person nor the world is changed by it. Sometimes circulating happens when we perceive and participate in an "eight to one" community that sustains and needs us. This may be a geographical or cultural community, one with common interests and passions, or a religious community. The key is not to go it alone, or to assume that our generosity is freelance.

We have found that one does not so much seek opportunities to circulate as recognize that giving or receiving for the right reason has a multiplying effect. In fact, overreaching to circulate may paradoxically deter the process, for the simple reason that it takes our eyes off the personal relationship that is the entry point for generosity. For circulating, our task is to wait consciously—and patiently—for the benefits, like interest in a savings account, to reveal themselves in due time.

READY TO SHARE

As generosity weaves its wonderful way through our lives, the needs around us, including the greatest needs of the world, inspire us to share. Japanese real estate tycoon Genshiro Kawamoto offered three of his multi-million-dollar homes in Hawaii to homeless and low-income families. One of these families was a single mother and her many daughters, who had lived in a shelter for five years. She wept as she received the keys. "What we need to do is appreciate," she said. Her response moved Kawamoto also to tears. On being asked about his "unusual venture" he responded simply that it made him happy.

We may struggle with concepts of heroic action—how much we can really do to help, or even whether we are capable—and then find that the call to share can come in a moment. From our own joy or suffering, illness, addictions, despair, healing, growth and maturity, we ultimately also need community to give resonance and depth to our experiences, to connect ourselves with the larger human story, and share with others that which defines us. We need to give ourselves as we are, so others can accept us as we are. We need to be able to receive others as they are in order to circulate to those who have known neither giving nor receiving. And we need to offer constancy and reliability as our foundation for doing so.

Once upon

～

TWO FAMILIES

She had suffered from bone cancer for a year
and was in unbearable pain. A young mother
with teenaged children, she lay in bed most
days, sleeping when she could, crying with
pain, occasionally watching television. Two
weeks before Christmas she saw a documentary about a family (parents out of work,
seven children trying to make something of
their lives with only their creativity to rely
on), and she couldn't believe it. Only two
hours from her, this family would have a
Christmas with no presents and no heat in
their rented house.

She phoned the TV network, tracked down
the producer and found the family. Her children, her husband and her friends began to purchase mittens and gloves, jackets, food, turkey,
chocolate treats and candy. She wanted only
new things, nothing used. She prepared baskets
of goodies with beautiful ribbons and paper. She
wrapped herself in a rug, grimacing with pain,

as her husband drove their laden car deep into the cold and barren countryside.

The family couldn't believe they'd come. They had received lots of promises from others and no one had delivered. The children smiled and showed their drawings pinned on the bare wall. They drank tea together and there were tears when they hugged each other farewell.

When the woman returned home, her pain worsened. She was admitted to hospital and died a month later. Her last giving had been to those in greater need. She had said that she had been loved, and had received abundance in her life. So she was glad to be able to share a small part of this with those who had little. Her friends were so moved by her example that they continued to support the family and formed a fund from the funeral donations to help others.

NB: A community of family is enhanced by circulating not only shared abundance but shared suffering. A deceased woman's love is kept alive by the continuous circulating love of friends.

As we have written earlier, acts of generosity, however small, are contagious. A book by Catherine Ryan Hyde, later made into a movie, proved the case for "paying it forward," by receiving some gift or courtesy and making the effort to pass the benefits or example on to unsuspecting others. The story is about the positive, even redemptive change that individuals realized from receiving random acts of intended kindness—sometimes quite extreme, like the giving of a car to a stranger. The protagonist in the story is a twelve-year-old, showing again that infectiousness multiplies when generosity is practised where it is least expected. Like the woman who cared for another family before herself dying, it may be a person facing terminal disease who somehow manages to see beyond her own suffering to be moved by that of others, thereby humbling, inspiring, healing and energizing those of us graced with health.

Other generous acts may come unsuspectedly when those who we presume have the least "pay forward" giving that is truly extravagant. Instead of being victim to life's harshness, the generous heart moves to the heroism of making life better for someone else. And, as is usually the case, the giver is enriched and renewed in the process of circulation. A person facing the end of life is at peace and complete after giving in ways that enrich the lives of others. A person carrying the wounds of cruelty and abuse overcomes these scars by sharing the lessons of suffering that may help relieve the suffering of others. Sharing becomes the foundation of circulating, by eliciting the willingness to give what we—and a community—need.

Once upon

A PRISONER

He had survived two years of persecution and, after an escape, he emigrated to Canada, where he married and landed a university teaching post. He loved his students but he wanted to do something in the community, something for the greater good.

One day a friend suggested he join a group at a prison visiting program. He hadn't realized how frightened he would be when he underwent inspection on entry. The hairs on his head stood on end at the clang of a security gate. He remembered the smell, the starvation, the humiliation. He looked into the eyes of the prisoners in the meeting room—he was not to know what it was they had done. He saw in their eyes the struggle of survival; he recognized them as lost family. After a year of volunteering, he became more active with the prison management. He demanded screens for toilets in the women's cells, he pushed for reform with overcrowding, he had telephones installed where there were none.

He eventually retired early from university to concentrate on making life better for the incarcerated. He knew how it was for them, and he wouldn't rest until he had contributed change, made it easier for them. And as he did this, groups began forming around him to help and to do the same in other prisons throughout the province.

NB: We are enabled through the generosity of a wounded heart. One person's suffering can awaken the compassion that leads to the healing of not one community but many.

We naturally wish to share ideas as well as experiences with others. This is why we need communities—not only to help others, but also to assist ourselves, to help us grow and change. This is especially important when it comes to our own artistry. Again, creativity is not something we look for, but something that comes to us. The more we practise generosity, the more we are open to the generosity of others. Michelangelo's dome atop St. Peter's Basilica in Rome is an excellent example of circulating. Employed by the pope, Michelangelo had produced vast artworks, such as those on the walls and ceiling of the Sistine Chapel. Near the end of his life, as construction on St. Peter's was proceeding apace, Michelangelo designed the dome as the crowning glory of the church. He donated this work as a creative act of worship and, in the sensibility of his time, for mercy for his past transgressions and errors. Michelangelo left a monument to his artistry and convictions for all to gaze upon. Even today, it defines Rome's skyline. It is magnificent, because of its grandeur, and because of the generosity behind its creation.

THE RIPPLE EFFECT

Writing a book is a long journey, usually done alone, and inevitably measured in outcomes such as chapters, drafts and revisions. Even though the aim is to engage readers, it is very easy in so prolonged a process to become too absorbed in the ideas or craft and therefore forget the relationship. We have learned that we need, as a constant priority, to be generous to our readers, and that such generosity has to begin with our own intentions. If we write only to make a living or to sell lots of books, then chances are we will have failed in producing something generative or stimulating. If we presume to be the authors of our own results, then, we have learned, we are in deep trouble for having neglected the possibilities of the cycle of giving, receiving and circulating before it has even begun. Our lesson is: start with the human being; then work back from there. Keep focused on the relationship; then let the art percolate.

Although it is usual to think the contrary, relationship is also the essence of money. As noted earlier, currency is a value that circulates with its own streams, patterns and values. Most of us work to earn money, but what we can buy with it depends on the value others perceive in the currency at large. Consider inflation: the paper does not change, nor does the unit—a dollar is still a dollar. What changes are perceptions. So in effect we all *hold* money more than own it. When we give money for goods or services, we are not simply in transaction but in a more vital exchange of promise, with the buyer assuring the worth of the payment, and the seller assuring the worth of what has been purchased. We do this so often that we can forget how all such commercial exchanges hinge on the very real generosity of trust.

Money, according to Italian activist and priest Arturo Paoli, links us together in community.

Paoli works among the poor in Latin America, and it would be easy for him to adopt the usual religious rhetoric and dismiss money as Mammon or the cause of greed and disparity. Instead, he teaches that money "is a symbol of life and a symbol of justice." As it enables making a living, money is essential to life. And when it circulates fairly, providing wages commensurate with effort, and making available equitably priced goods, money distributes justice. Just as humans have the right to breathe, each person has a right to participate in the circulation of money because it enables aspects of our freedom—to choose what we desire, to go where we think best, to buy what we need or to invest towards what we hope. Paoli raises the dignity of money to remind us to respect its power. In healthy circulation with everyone participating, money is life-giving. If instead money is hoarded, the stymied circulation causes the same injury or death to the body of the community as would happen to a human body with oxygen or blood restricted and blocked. Paoli goes so far as to call money *grace*, by which he means that it is a means for individuals to exchange goodness. Like anything else, we can distort or stunt or reject this grace by insisting it is ours alone. Then it atrophies. Or we can accept the grace as a gift, relish its possibilities and realize that potential by passing it on.

Communities that do not circulate become bureaucracies. In his study of over one hundred philanthropic foundations, American researcher and writer Joel Fleishman compiled a type of balance sheet of assets and liabilities. On the one hand, foundations have realized considerable social benefits, including creating nationwide systems for emergency phone numbers, and seeding the micro-credit innovations that made possible the Grameen Bank. Both of these are examples of investments in circulation that generated opportunities for millions of people. On the other hand, foundations all too often fail in their purpose, sometimes by stubbornly persisting with projects that are not working or are unethical, or through "an inappropriate level of secrecy and even arrogance." Denying failure (the equivalent of not being able to say "I'm sorry") is a withdrawal from circulation, as is secrecy. As Fleishman points out, the foundation sector "seriously underperforms its potential."

By implication, even organizations such as foundations or charities, which are constituted for generosity, must continue to learn how to be generous. The means for what Fleishman and others call "transparency" and "accountability" is nothing more than a commitment to the spirit and practices of circulation.

Circulating our abundance and good fortune, with the right intentions, is always generous. One example that has touched us is Yoko Ono's recent gift of John Lennon's solo songbook to Amnesty International, which will record it with volunteer artists as a means of fundraising for Amnesty's work upholding human rights around the world. The giving is of Lennon's artistry, the receiving by Amnesty brings with it a new resource for its generative work. Yet the value is far beyond that literal exchange. We await the new cluster of musicians who will interpret these songs and enliven them for our time.

All of us have something to offer from our receiving that spins, spirals and circulates into the world with and beyond us. Norwegian athlete Johann Olav Koss led the Right to Play movement, which grew out of the social investment

strategy of the Lillehammer Olympics in 1994.
The core idea is to spread peace, health and
belonging by bringing possibilities of involvement in sport to boys and girls around the world,
particularly where poverty and HIV/AIDS have
prevented any hope. Many athletes have volunteered time and funds to support Koss in his mission. Our friend Eric Young developed the now
world-famous red soccer ball that has become the
icon for Right to Play. Thousands of balls, distributed to desperate communities, are inscribed
with the circulating motto "Take care of yourself.
Take care of each other."

The Right to Play movement became a much
wider social phenomenon at the Torino Winter
Olympics in 2006. American speed skater Joey
Cheek shifted the mood of the Olympics—and of
its worldwide spectators—from applauding the
winning to witnessing generosity at play. Cheek
donated his $25,000 prize from his gold medal to
Right to Play. As U.S. corporations jumped on the
bandwagon, many private donors followed suit.
But the most warming of all giving was that of
Canadian gold speed skater Clara Hughes. There
are no financial prizes for Canadian athletes, yet

Hughes—inspired by Cheek and wanting to make her win a gift to others for all she had received—offered her own personal money, $10,000, to Right to Play. Once again, corporations followed that lead, pledging another $200,000, and private donors also poured in their support, challenged by Hughes's example. This generative circulating represents authentic generosity and exemplifies, in a dramatic way, some of the key virtues. How rare that, in a moment of personal achievement, realizing years of sacrifice, drive and ambition, Hughes retained the *humility* to appreciate all the gifts and givers who had helped her succeed. How rare that, in the most competitive of realms, she had the heart and consciousness to *discern* what would give her win an even higher significance—that she would, in a moment, pass it on to those with greater needs, and share her joy of her sport.

There are several lessons in this. First, we tend to think that sports, business and life itself are defined by competition, with an exclusive focus on winning at almost all cost. Human beings in fact are constituted differently. Even in moments of ultimate triumph the honest heart recognizes the interdependencies that made such personal accomplishment possible. No person can stand out alone, even—especially—when standing on a gold-medal podium. Second, the world hungers for examples of generosity, and readily follows those who set the example. We all need *courage* and *discernment;* we all have capacities for *mercy* and risk taking. Exemplars lift us to try, in our own way, what we know to be right and possible. Third, we all have moments that can turn complacency into generosity, when our choices, words or actions can provoke others to follow our lead and invest, even in some small way, in our shared humanity.

Neither of us is an Olympic athlete, yet we found ourselves on a stage of sorts for circulating when we discovered a ceaseless spring of fresh water on our Italian property after we purchased it. How lucky were we! All we had to do was get a pipe and pump, and we had as much water as we could possibly need. A few months after we moved in, a man from the large, rambling property not far from us arrived at our gate with a challenging request. After the neighbourly niceties, he asked for access to this water. He explained that they had none on their property, they were too far in the country to be served by the community system, and he had always known about our spring but had been denied water from it by previous owners. We pondered his request, went through the usual dilemmas, and wondered about the peculiar Italian laws that we had discovered often make it easy for trespassers to claim squatters' rights. If we share the water, we asked ourselves, will there be enough for us? What are potential implications of acceding to his request to dig out and bury a pipe through our field and along our driveway? We had been warned to be very private and protective—indeed suspicious—for, as outsiders, we were fair game for clever locals. Yet he was our neighbour, and we were meant to be Christian, so how could we not challenge our hesitation to share this precious—and coveted—resource?

We finally entered into an agreement with him that he could have the water free of charge (as we had received it), which surprised him (and many other neighbours who eventually learned of our gift). Baskets of fruit began arriving from people we had never met, from far away from our valley.

This story circulated in town, six kilometres away, where some people viewed us as foolish foreigners. But many took our act to be a sign of our commitment to the community. Unbeknownst to us, this water was a much bigger issue than simply supplying our neighbour's house. It came to supply four families who shared the same rambling building. Again this is a literal circulating, in that the water has been on our property for centuries, and will likely be there long after us. We all have an abundance of this water—more than enough for all our needs, including watering rows of flowers and legions of lawns. We feel we did the right thing—we practised what we believed, to share with those who had less—even though it was a risk, and still is. And our neighbourhood lives and thrives on what the Earth has given us all in a hamlet in Tuscany.

From our challenges sharing water we learned of our neighbour's astonishment. He hadn't expected us to agree to share it. We learned that surprise is contagious. Generosity given and received, when least expected, generates generosity—a ripple effect far further than the giver could imagine.

The Generous Question: What Do You Need?

As the four most generous words are "thank you" and "I'm sorry," then the most generous question is "What do you need?" This we found to be the only generous question to ask anyone—including oneself—and any community as part of one's entry into it. What is the need? You cannot second-guess someone's need—you may have an idea but you cannot know the full truth unless you ask. "What do you need?" is also the most generous question to ask someone who is sick or dying. The answer can surprise us. A lot of people who have less than we do don't necessarily want what we have. They don't necessarily need money, either. It takes risk to ask the generous question. You may not like what you hear in reply but the truth is released in its asking, and the truth is what we all need.

Sometimes those asked the generous question do not know how to answer it, usually because no one has ever asked them. Under these circumstances, it is generous not to try to answer it for them, but to keep asking the question until they can answer it themselves. This is where a break-through can happen.

Once upon

A TELEVISION

As a grassroots group of women formed to help women in need, they received a phone call from a young mother from Somalia, recently arrived in Canada.

A volunteer went to the apartment in which she was staying; it took hours by bus to get there. They met in the room where the young woman lived with her three-year-old daughter.

"What do you need?" the volunteer asked the mother.

"A TV. If I have a TV then I can keep my girl quiet. They complain all the time in the apartment about her making noise. I am afraid they'll throw us out."

"What else do you need?" she asked her. The woman looked shocked. A TV was what she thought she needed.

"Well, a bed. This one sags and hurts my back."

"What else do you need?"

"Well"—a smile broke out on her face—"I'd like a chair so we don't have to sit on the bed all the time."

"And what else do you need?"

And so the answers came and a list emerged.

On returning home, the volunteer noticed her next-door neighbour carrying a TV out of his house and putting it on the front lawn. "I've just bought a digital one, so this has to go," he said.

"Does it work?" she asked.

"Oh yes," he replied.

"Then I'll have it. I have just the place for it and it isn't the garbage!" She told him about the woman's need, and he got in his car and delivered the TV that evening.

Within the week the woman had had all her needs met. Everything she had asked for had been given by others and delivered by members of the community. The young woman felt renewed and confident. She hardly believed that she had been helped in the way she had experienced. She wanted to start her own group among Somalian immigrant women. She wanted to practise giving, receiving and circulating.

And she did. She moved from her room to her own apartment, her daughter got into day-care, and she set up a fund to help those in her community receive what they needed to move them out of despair, to hope and a life enhanced by the practice of generosity.

NB: Asking the generous question not once but many times provides the opportunity to practise "double and" in filling up a person's need to excess, not just providing the basics. This, in turn, allows the recipient to immediately circulate instead of just receive. And the ripple effect begins.

Generous Communication

Every task or project can be done with generosity, or not. So too, every word spoken or written can be generative, or not. As mentioned, we try as writers to be not only aware of our readers but also generous to them. We strive for clarity and honesty to share understanding, and also to provoke questions we have not asked or raise issues other than those we have covered. This is a dialogue: we have learned from others and now we hope that learning will spread and circulate as the ideas are taken up and added to by others. The concept of generosity in writing is something that we learned especially from Edwina Vardey, and hence the reason we have co-dedicated this book to her.

A diarist all her life—even while bringing up five children and extending a home to her widowed mother—she would note the activities and sayings of her children on a daily basis. When they each reached twenty-one, she composed a book of these quotes particular to them, with letters and other memorabilia from their childhood. A Red Cross naval nurse in the Second World War, she wrote diaries of such quality and detail that historians and documentary makers reference them as a resource for studying a woman's experience over a span of decades. Trained as a book editor, Edwina had a love of history and an interest in the lives of people, past and present, that led her to compile the definitive history (from the Mesolithic Age onward) of her adopted town in Surrey, England. She interviewed senior residents and drew from them the highlights of what they perceived as an uneventful life. These audiotapes are now invaluable to the local History Society, as these people's lives, as in a mosaic, tell the history of a place.

Still very active, Edwina offers creative writing classes in her home to retired local people. She helps develop their confidence—and therefore their risk taking as writers—so that they can publish (some have won literary awards) and read their works, selected by her, at an annual reading in the nearby bookstore. The Penny Readings was an idea Edwina resurrected from Victorian times; residents would gather in community to listen to the creativity of others. Edwina also turns her talent of pulling the best out of what seems an ordinary life to writing encapsulated biographies of members of her parish congregation in its bulletin. It is not simply that she is good with words, she is also generous with them, using her craft as a writer and skills as a teacher to give voice to others in the community. Through her many letters and cards over the years, Edwina fills others with hope, and a youthful inspiration. She's an example of living life to the fullest by circulating generosity and creativity.

Like generosity itself, circulating is really neither an option nor a personal choice. It is already a living, dynamic reality that surrounds, supports and envelops our personal human reality, whether we are conscious of this or not, whether we are responsive or not. The most pressing danger to our human possibilities is not from *not* giving, but from taking circulating for granted.

One of our most promising technological achievements is the Internet. While it is largely self-governing, and certainly heavy with human potential, much of the functionality of this now vital tool for global communication and community making is being stifled by reams of spam, threatened by destructive viruses, and in many ways monopolized by what some experts believe to be the most profitable e-business of all time— pornography. Such non-generative dissemination abuses circulation and carries an even deadlier virus, that of broken dignity, exploitation, abuse and isolation. Research has indicated that the most obsessive on-line users are also among the loneliest—endlessly searching, shopping and chatting without ever making community.

Paradoxically, the technology of connection does not always bring people closer together, and the bandwidth for much more information does very little to improve understanding. For connecting to become community hinges on the generosity with which we give, receive and circulate what really matters. To become generous Internet users ourselves, we might consider what we circulate to our mailing lists of colleagues and friends. Is it an outreach for relationship or just an easy mode for downloading unrelated ideas and information? Are we giving what we need to receive when communicating this way? Are we doing unto others what we, ourselves, would wish done to us?

The Internet as a tool is not an end in itself. French Jesuit scientist Pierre Teilhard de Chardin has been called the "father of the Internet" for envisioning fifty years ago a globe-straddling and shared human consciousness. Indeed, there are many examples of groups using the Internet to share work, resources and wisdom, especially in solving intractable problems of homelessness, poverty and abuse. Our generosity, as individuals, has been greatly magnified by our inclusion in this circulation of needs and ideals. We need to be aware of using this generous facility with respect for each other (especially with the words and greetings we use), and with awareness of enhancing relationship (especially when replying to "all"). By stepping into this stream of community—whether as small as "eight to one" or as large as a global network—we can more fully appreciate the interconnections within which we do our giving along with our receiving.

SEVEN

The Art of the Heart

GENEROSITY practised consistently, through giving, receiving and circulating, not only lives as an art unto itself but also can be the perfect foundation for creating a centred and purposeful way of life. Generosity embraced becomes the defining aspect of one's character, permeating and unifying all that we are, all that we do, think, speak and feel. Integrity lives within our generosity, a wholeness that is consistent, reliable and humble; a giving that is *compassionate*, *merciful* and *hope* inducing. Receiving that is rich in *discernment* appreciates what is enabled and fuels the *courage* for regeneration. And circulating is premised on *remembering* our histories and "her-stories" to serve the wisdom of our past as we invest *trust* in the present towards a beauty of *balance*. Giving, receiving and circulating is not so much a skill set to be mastered as it is a blueprint for the workings of the human heart. If we use our heads to try to decipher the workings of generosity, we'll fail. Our experience is that you can't come to generosity through purely intellectual understanding, but you can come to understanding by practising generosity.

As generosity comes alive through experience, our hearts need to be alert, attentive and open to activate and sustain it. Giving, receiving and circulating does, at some point in practice, become fused in not only one's own heart but also the greater heart of being, circling its harmonies and cacophonies around and within us. If we monitor our hearts in defining our actions, then we will not be pulled from a circular cycle onto a straight and linear path towards the hazardous contradiction of self-serving righteousness.

Giving, receiving and circulating is a way of life; it gathers the ten virtues of generosity—*courage, discernment, humility, compassion, mercy, reliability, trust, hope, remembering and balance*—into a collective form of loving expression.

In this chapter we explore some practicalities of living generously along with the challenges that face us as practitioners.

CULTIVATING A GENEROUS ATTITUDE

Whatever the circumstances, whatever the call for action—or inaction for that matter—it is vital to foster a generous attitude towards everything, everyone and yourself. This generous attitude involves a constancy of the heart, a choice of loving understanding over hurtful judgment and removed separation. It is to put what Mother Teresa defined as love into action. Action is not thought, it is behaviour; love in action is therefore the behaviour of the heart *in relationship.*

To gauge the power of the heart, we can and must learn from the examples of those who chose to be generous in the darkest times. Our age is still in the shadow of the Holocaust, because of the enormity of that annihilation; however, genocides are still happening. Concepts of human morality, such as generosity, need to answer to such failures in compassion and mercy. As human beings we need to face two truths. First, as scholars and historians continue to show, one regime, the Nazis, perpetrated the Holocaust, but many countries share responsibility for the scale of the tragedy. Countries within Europe persecuted Jews before the Nazi invasion, and all too readily gave away the Jewish members of their communities for deportation to concentration camps. Countries outside Europe, including Canada, the United States and Australia, blocked immigrants and refugees knowing that those being turned away were being condemned to inhuman fates. The opposite of generosity is not an inconsiderable thing, so the first truth is that *complacency in the face of injustice carries its own culpability.*

The second truth is that *generosity practised in the most "degenerative" environments can profoundly change the terms and experience of that reality, reversing even the most oppressive hate into opportunities for love and hope.* Stories of heroic

acts in moments of despair nourish our own
hearts in the hearing. For instance, we have been
moved by the writings and subsequent witness
accounts of Jewish philosopher and Carmelite
nun Edith Stein, who took it on herself to care for
many in a holding camp in Holland, where she
was imprisoned with innumerable mothers and
children. Understandably, many couldn't cope
with the horror, squalor and inhumanity of the
surroundings. Edith practised a simple, gentle
love, offering the smallest courtesies, looking
after children whose mothers were incapacitated
by fear, consoling even while sharing in the abject
desolation. Her loving example persisted not only
throughout the internment at the holding camp,
but also through the long days and nights aboard
the freight trains as they travelled to the ovens of
Auschwitz. Edith was exterminated, but not her
spirit, nor her generous loving heart.

Another inspiring soul who perished in the
Holocaust is Etty Hillesum, a young Jewish
lawyer who kept a diary (now published) of her
experiences in a camp. Etty did not wait to be
arrested; she actually brought food, clothes and
kindness to people rounded up and imprisoned

before the Nazi bureaucracy caught up with her. She exemplified so much *courage* in choosing to serve instead of run, and *compassion* in risking personal exposure so to reach out to her suffering community. In the journals and letters to friends that she wrote during her imprisonment, Etty shared many of the dilemmas of faith and hope. She challenged herself to see God—and therefore the good—in the faces of those who guarded and often abused her. She struggled to *discern* the aspects of beauty that the drabness of the prison tried to destroy, writing in wonder about a jasmine plant blooming just beyond the barbed wire. And she reminded herself to "dare to speak the name of God," as a practice meshing *remembering* and *hope*.

Like Edith Stein, Etty Hillesum was tireless in ministering to those most traumatized around her. In her writings we read about how she appointed herself the barracks' "thinking heart." What an immense heart it must have been to be capable of these terms of generosity—to give when she herself was in such need, to receive grace and beauty even when they were so impossible to recognize. Thus she circulated her generosity through the horrors of the past for our present benefit.

A "thinking heart" is the perfect organ for generosity. Most of the time we separate mind from heart, reason from emotion. When they are combined, as they were by Etty, the result is *balanced* action—a need to fulfill our yearning for relationship, belonging and even spiritual transcendence, despite the animosity, disequilibrium and suffering. With a thinking heart we come to understanding from participating rather than just figuring it out. We come to give what is needed, or relish what is received, and circulate with compassion. Etty, Edith and other indisputable heroes of that dark time, such as Dietrich Bonhoeffer, had the clarity to stand at the precipice of evil, and insist on not only believing in the good, but also doing the right thing. This is the insistence that generosity aims to emulate: giving life where it is most needed, pulling people from their darkness to glimpse moments of light, and bringing hope and mercy to lives in the face of hopelessness and dejection.

We may wonder how we can be "thinking hearts" in our comfortable realities. The truth is that opportunity arrives every day. It may be to thoughtfully refine your attitude to always turn to generosity. It may be for you to extend your heart and be generous where you have been least welcome. It may be to practise a constancy of generosity, with open head and open heart, where it is most lacking, especially within workplaces or in times of trial within families. It may be to learn the art of adopting generous language—of expressing gratitude, contrition and appreciation, or asking what another needs and being part of delivering it. If we remember that enabling another is a generous act of the heart, if we take time to be with a person who has less than us—be that material, emotional or intellectual—we will learn the art of the heart in action.

We always have a choice to think generously and to act generously, and when we choose generosity we contribute to the treasure of life in ways we may not see or cannot even imagine. We may not be in prison. We may not be facing a death sentence. But in our own ways, we can confront what dehumanizes and help generate what adds beauty to a world in need.

In order to do this—to discern the generous way—it is essential to ask ourselves again whether our decisions and our contributions are about us or about another. Is it concerning me or concerning someone else? This is the orienting question, the monitor of pure intention and the test for a thinking heart. This is the question to filter our actions, so we do not get caught in the damaging zones of manipulative generosity (conditional), strategic generosity (exchange), boomerang generosity (how much I will get back?), cosmetic generosity (look how good I am) or false generosity (giving to fulfill obligations), which do not circulate and therefore degenerate. We cannot practise giving, receiving and circulating without being taken over by the circularity and interdependence that a thinking heart discerns. If we give from a false, or uninformed, or hasty perspective; if we receive without connecting to the broader possibilities involved; or if we miss the hope circulating around us, we will find it almost impossible to participate in authentic generosity. Then we will confuse and sometimes hurt people along the way, including ourselves.

As we have found in our own lives, and have illustrated with many examples and stories, practising generosity is not necessarily an easy path. We must be honest and acknowledge that there are undertows, undersides and dysfunctions even as we commit ourselves to what seems to be a good cause or motivation. One incident that left a sour taste in our mouths was being asked for a sizable loan by some acquaintances for "just a few months." They were moving and were stressed by everything around them. Once they left we had no contact. Months passed, then years, including times when our own finances could have used the fairly large sum we had lent. Five years later an e-mail arrived, with a promise to begin repaying the loan in instalments over two years, which was a relief to us but hardly a generative completion. We had, in hindsight, given out of our heartfelt empathy but with too little thoughtful discernment.

While the difficulty around such situations is real, we have also learned that most of our giving has been beneficial to others. Struggling to allow our hearts to think has enriched our marriage and enhanced our work. It has become the manner in which we choose to meet others and the world, sharing in grief without becoming frozen by it, and giving ourselves to human hope without becoming burned out. Even when we make mistakes—for instance, giving too quickly without thinking of our needs as well as the needs of the recipient—a thinking heart has helped us to heal from the experience while also discovering insights and even threads of precious wisdom. Once again, if we hold fast to the virtues that comprise true generosity, then the ground is secure for walking upon. Here is a brief reminder with some additional advice:

Courage—be clear-headed and calm-hearted
Discernment—be wise, listening to the heart as
    well as the head
Humility—be open-hearted and open-minded
Compassion—be caring
Mercy—be careful
Reliability—be constant
Trust—be surrendered and forgiving
Hope—be resourceful and joyful
Remembering—be honouring
Balance—be flexible between head and heart.

Small Everyday Things with
Big Consequences

As with physical exercise and good nutrition, we can measure the results of a healthy generosity by practising its forms consistently and with patience. We understand the need to go slowly for the long-term result. Exercising a thinking heart requires a similar regimen. Doing small things generously every day makes a big cumulative difference. More than that, doing small things caringly over time prepares us to be ready and willing to participate when big-time generosity is demanded. These small yet ultimately transformative practices include the following.

1. LOOK

Learn to look differently and see anew. See with gratitude, and see with compassion what others need. Again, the line from the prayer of St. Francis, "Let us not so much seek to be understood as to understand," is a helpful guide for learning to see generously by noticing others. Generosity requires us to receive the goodness of others in our giving, to look for that goodness in even the most unlikely places. Then, instead of judging, gossiping, complaining or worrying about how people are towards themselves or ourselves or others, we can step into appreciating them for what it is that is right, unique and fine about them. Somehow when we do this we begin our own conversion to seeing generously.

2. APPRECIATE

Relish what we receive yet often take for granted. Respect those who give yet whose gifts we take for granted. Be thankful for every relational exchange. When we are so present with others we are appreciating them. When we appreciate them we are giving them life, filling them with the natural confidence of being seen. Our core human desire is to be seen as who we are, not only truthfully but also with appreciation. As we are all vulnerable, we need to hear these appreciations and know that we have been seen and heard, not once but all the time. As generosity has taught us, we need to be reliable in our gratitude—our thank-yous and our appreciations—reliable in our support, reliable in friendship and reliable in our expression.

Remember too to give what it is we need to receive without expectations of a response—even an acknowledgment. To receive appreciations from others takes time, but we have found that this is always time well spent. Appreciating others is not undertaken as a courtesy or *quid pro quo*. Instead we give appreciations every day.

> *NB: If you delay appreciating someone, you lose the window of generosity. Delayed appreciation— like delayed forgiveness—creates in its absence more sorrow and hurt in the person being dismissed. It is never too late to appreciate, but generosity requires us to do it the moment we experience it, face to face, or in a card or e-mail. If we put appreciation on a list of things to do later, or leave it until a person's deathbed or funeral, then we risk having to live with the double regret of what has remained unsaid and unresolved for both.*

3. LISTEN

Hear what is meant as well as what is said. Silence the distraction of what your mind wants to say to truly hear what needs to be heard. A hasty response to a need, without listening, is not always generous. If a situation is not appropriate for asking the generous question, "What do you need?" at least, as generous practitioners, we ourselves need to practise the art of listening. Because only by truly listening to a person will we discern the real or deeper need that is often masked by what is asked for. If we listen with our hearts then we find the truth. To truthfully listen is to hear what is being said or done. This will help us in continuing to be consciously generous amid sometimes hurtful challenges.

4. LEARN

We are all forever students of generosity. As with any wisdom, we must welcome the insights by being open to the challenge they pose. We must honour what others teach us. We must keep alive the childish curiosity that keeps us humble before all that we will never really know and understand. The lessons learned in choosing generosity as a way of life are varied. We have found that if you choose generosity in every situation, then you learn how generosity can heal not only yourself but others within the situation.

We both have learned that:

- Generosity is always contagious. When we have been, or others have been for us, examples of consistent generosity, the gift beyond the giving is that it helps teach others to find a positive way of being.
- The most powerful antibody for the epidemic of fear and suspicion is the courage to challenge the status quo through love in action.
- There are daily attempts to thwart generosity that come from hardened and hurt hearts (all too often including our own).
- The thwarting that most damages the prospects of circulating comes from criticisms (including the conventions of critique and cynicism prominent in today's academia and in journalism).
- Pressures for productivity at work push us off balance, and this now normalized imbalance not only curtails giving but also keeps us away from enjoyment of all the blessings we have actually received.

- Rushing to beat time, jostling for breathing space on the roads and in lineups, leaves little if any room for real encounter, accommodation or companionship.

Once upon

⁓

A GRANDMOTHER

It had been going on too long. Her daughter, addicted to drugs, was never home. Her two grandchildren were becoming unruly. Their father had run off.

She wanted so much for her daughter to be healed but all the prayers, all the letters, all the visits to detox centres hadn't worked. Now she had to step in again, to take care of her grandchildren.

She went to court and adopted them. Her daughter swore at her, accused her of taking her only joys. She went ahead anyway, flew them back from the west coast and began a life of babysitting, driving to schools, camps and baseball practice. She became a mom again.

Tired and in her fifties, she found her part-time job insufficient for their needs, but friends helped and people gave her little extras that made the difference—support, money at Christmas, even a new mortgage on the house—and somehow she managed. She knew what she was doing was the right thing.

The years passed and, as the children grew, she still wondered every day about her daughter. The phone call she dreaded came one afternoon. Her daughter was lost on the streets. She knew she had to do something, go into action. Supported by prayers from her community, she flew out to the city and scoured the rougher districts. On the third day she found her daughter, near death, slumped against a bin. She called her name and as their eyes met, her sobbing daughter reached out her arms.

She took care of her daughter in the hotel and then offered her the airfare home. They flew back together, and her daughter entered a centre near the family. United with her children, she is slowly piecing her life together, seeing hope in the love of her mother. Her mother is seeing the fruit of her love and sacrifices in a united family.

NB: Don't give up, give.

~

UNLEARNING

Looking, appreciating, listening and learning point us to what is possible, but may not, in themselves, be enough. We may also need to disentangle our presumptions or automatic reactions, and peel away past attitudes that prevent true generosity from spreading through us. This process of "unlearning" is, according to the medieval scholar and philosopher St. Bonaventure, the initial step towards wisdom. As a couple, we have found that the most obdurate challenges usually require some degree of unlearning. When changing careers, for example, we had to unlearn the harsh schedules of managing to be effective in the flexibility and flow of creativity. The following are a few lessons, gained from our experience, that exemplify what may need to be unlearned to uncork or regenerate generosity:

1. WITHHOLDING

Keeping back. Keeping apart. Keeping distance. One of us, who is shy, admits that what feels like a natural attribute of personality is also a mechanism for withholding self from another, which can sometimes harden into ungenerous, egocentric behaviour. Shyness (the one who is not shy points out) prevents us from sharing ourselves, and from exercising the courage to put love into action. Through shyness we sometimes remove ourselves from others as a form of protection from some imaginary threat, or to protect the "I'm not good enough" belief system. In the process we prevent giving, receiving and circulating anything by bringing attention only to our shyness, which contributes to awkwardness in others, and denies them the freedom to give. A generous way of being is to break the fear of self by letting go of self-conceptions and starting to look towards others' needs.

Forgetting is another form of withholding. It is a choice to not remember, and its message to a recipient is that he or she is not worth honouring, and is disrespected. Genuinely forgetting anniversaries or birthdays can occasionally be forgiven, but it is almost the stereotype for an ungenerous life, a life too full of activities other than perhaps the ones that matter most. Forgetting to think of those who are friends or colleagues also shows that too much time is taken thinking of oneself. Not remembering someone's name makes the individual feel less a person. The generous way to respond to those who are forgetful of you is to constantly remember them instead, therefore practising giving what you need to receive.

Not taking care of details is another withholding of generosity. Be they small daily details or larger ones of life, ignoring one's own responsibility in details puts stress on—and frequently exhausts—those who don't ignore them. For instance, not making sure that a will is in place for your estate, leaving your life in a mess for someone else—or many people—to clear up, is not practising generosity at all. So is turning a blind eye to emotional matters that you don't have the courage or clarity to deal with. Clearing conflict is an act of generosity. Clearing up a life is an act of generosity. Clearing up personality issues through therapy is an act of generosity. Putting what matters on hold hurts the heart.

2. DEFICITS AND ABUSES

Refusing to change. Refusing to take the action that is necessary. Preferring the certainty of not having enough, or not giving enough, rather than taking the risk to circulate. Living one's life in situations that are abusive—be they self-abusive (e.g., addictions), or abuses from others (e.g., domestic violence, or staying in an abusive workplace or friendship or relationship)—is ultimately ungenerous to one's self and others. A generous friend who listens to your woes can do so for only a limited time. Endless listening without any action taken by the abused only contributes to the abuse. Taking a listener's time by constantly talking about a problem abuses that person's empathy and emotions.

Similarly, endless giving ceases to be extraordinary. Rather than being generative, such giving, if out of guilt, inadequacy or narcissism, invariably only perpetuates an abusive situation. In this sense, constant giving is but a form of co-dependency. This is ungenerous to not only oneself but also others, because it isn't giving, receiving and circulating, nor is it relational. It is usually a manipulative and even dangerous palliative.

Endless taking is abusive not only to systems of generosity but also to people who are generous. Taking from others' generosity in excess is a passive-aggressive form of abuse. A person who lacks responsibility for his or her life and expects others to provide for every need is not abusive if a genuine need results from a life trauma. However, if the need is endless, and has become a way of life, it ruins any lesson of the heart and closes all possibilities for active generosity. Appreciation is usually lacking.

The generous response to people unable to give, receive or circulate is to help provide them opportunities for giving to others who have less. This shift in focus from their own plight stirs awareness that we all share some suffering and can do something to relieve it.

3. RIGIDITY

We all have assumptions, which sometimes can be brutally inflexible. Being rigid, in either ideology or opinions, or being closed towards others because of their differences, is not only unhealthy for generosity but also breeds its opposite, which is the fear-induced refusal to give, the refusal to receive, and the isolation-reinforcing refusal to circulate. Rigidity is rampant when we stay the same ("I'm OK as I am" or "I'm already a good person") or default to ideological simplicities ("I already know what is right and why everyone else is wrong").

Part of the challenge of generously alleviating the loneliness around us is to work to dissolve the underlying rigidity. It may not be in our power to influence the change. But, as the Quakers teach, this is not enough reason not to give anyway. From their long history of peace activism, justice work and visitation to prisons, the Quakers have learned that being present even for what clearly seems to be a lost cause still has significance and consequence. Insisting on hope in the face of despair or standing as a witness to love in the face of hatred circulates even when the subjects of giving or receiving seem unresponsive or unmoved.

4. THE NEVER-ENOUGH EVASION

People who complain about not having enough—time, money, energy, opportunities—too often make their complaining central in their life, and become real drains on their friends and families. When we convince ourselves that we have too little to give, we by default become generosity "black holes," sucking up the energy and attention of those around us who care. We have found that when the complainer complains about never having enough, the listeners become one-way sounding boards who are never particularly asked about their needs. A sounding board is not so much receiving or circulating because usually the person doing the sounding simply expects to hear back the echo of what he or she already thinks or believes.

Another gentle abuse from busyness occurs when we do not have enough time to think through a problem, and ask friends or colleagues if we can "pick their brains." The premise, as the language suggests, is a form of theft. Rather than relationship or co-questioning, there is only a taking from another of what is most needed or valuable. People who are chronic "brain pickers" see their own busyness, yet fail to recognize the time burdens on those being picked. The rush does not blind us to what we want, but it does often make us insensitive to those from whom we need.

5. PINCHING

When giving to those who ask, it is always a challenge when they can—and many times do— come back for more. Once isn't enough, one amount of money won't do. The presumption here is that obviously you—the generous person—"have more than me, so I will ask for more." And "Since you have agreed to give, I've probably not yet got all that may be available to me." Both of us have experienced this double-take several times, from individuals, and from causes or other NGOs. In "thank you" letters from charities we are often gratefully acknowledged for what we have given and in the same letter asked to give again. Of course, we recognize the ongoing need. But knowing where to draw the line involves respect for the process of circulating. Everything has its cycle, with thanks and appreciations needing to get their full due, not to be quick courtesies as part of getting more.

In the case of personal requests for money, we have learned that if a person in need has asked for a loan, it is usually better to give the money than to be involved in haphazard methods of repayment. Sometimes the need alone deserves the offering, and the repayment becomes only another dynamic of co-dependence. When we have been generous only to find that our giving has been dismissed or minimized by further requests, we have had to discern how we feel, and clarify our response according to our needs and criteria as also receivers and circulators.

6. GREED

Throughout history, greed has usually been regarded as a vice. Only recently has this changed. Society on the whole is now more ambiguous towards greed. Investment companies, market analysts and bankers make the case that, in fact, greed is good. This economic justification has in many ways crept into culture at large, and obliterated any conditions or constraints. MTV and

MuchMusic have popular series about the ostentatious lifestyle of rock and rap stars. The music still matters, but the ethos is as much about the "bling" as the art. However we regard such over-the-top displays of wealth, the fact is that few of us are exempt from the attitudes that drive our markets, elevate our celebrities, form our culture and shape our values. Perhaps the most difficult task for a thinking heart is to pierce this now dominant justification for greed, to be honest about its real costs, and to be truthful about how greed has infiltrated our own perspective and expectations. It is not just the rich who subscribe to "shop till you drop"; it is not just those who have the most who seem to have a hard time sharing.

Greed basically handcuffs generosity in three ways. It usually forgets or neglects giving. It also does not so much receive as take, which means that entitlement and accumulation have complete precedence over any sense of proportion, or any sense of relishing. Greed, by definition, stockpiles rather than circulates. Many people work hard at what they do, and deserve the rewards of that hard work. But the generosity suppressed when greed is dominant constrains their own lives. Hoarding is as much an impulse of fear as one of possessing. So when we are out of the stream of generosity's circulation, while we may be self-sufficient, the absence of circulating often leaves us unsatisfied. Greed can never be the basis for community. It can never satisfy the claims and possibilities of love.

AT HOME IN THE HEART

We are at home in the heart of the art of generosity when we experience a certain freedom and detachment from outcomes. This detachment, an interior attitude, is where others' lack of generosity doesn't deter our own practice of it, nor are we caught up in expecting something from someone in return. To maintain this detachment we need to protect our hearts, to remain clear and constant in our generous ideas, attitudes and actions. Otherwise we may doubt our own responses and fall back into old methods of being. We may have infrequent support in our being generous. Those nearest us may be the ones who most challenge our insistence to give, receive, circulate and change. As we have noted earlier, our changing, our generosity, may threaten others in their unchecked assumptions or complacencies. Under these circumstances, the very real art of generosity is to hold others' hurt close to our own hearts, knowing well that these are not our injuries but theirs. Walking with loving thoughts or prayer towards those who hurt us is practising not only the virtue of *mercy,* but the process of "foregiveness." To give ahead, to fore-give, is to see the goodness in another before and beyond the hurts that may be committed or endured. The process of fore-giving is to liberate oneself from being hurt by another's hurts, and to enable others to be loved anyway, forgiven for their mistakes and errors, the way we would wish to be. This proactive giving—giving before or forgiving in advance—is one of the highest acts of circulation.

Once upon

⌒

A FORE-GIVE

Her younger sister had had a hard life. Hers had been blessed. She knew that her sister held grudges against her. She was always so angry, so dismissive, so rude to her. Yet she was all she had.

One day she fell and broke her hip. Her younger sister was too busy to help her—get someone else, one of your neighbours, she suggested. After surgery, she held no grudge, she didn't expect any change. That was the way it was. Then her sister became ill—she didn't need any help, thank you. But she went anyway and cared for her. She didn't expect any change in her attitude towards her, and there wasn't any.

It was on the anniversary of their mother's death that she called her younger sister on the phone to commiserate. Her sister responded that she was too busy—don't be so sentimental, she said. She put down the phone. That's it, she thought, why bother? But before she took her own advice, she knew it wouldn't help. They had only each other.

So she redialed. Her sister was surprised that she'd called back and equally surprised at the invitation to lunch the next day—for no reason than just to be together.

As they ate, her younger sister recounted the hardships of her life, her regrets and resentments. When they finished a bottle of wine they found themselves smiling. It was good to be together, even for a short while.

NB: Don't give up, give.

⁓

Beyond trying again, we also have a responsibility to practise the generous art of correction when we have been the recipient of an attack, or in the absence of gratitude or apology. This is not an exercise in "I am right and you are wrong," but one of thinking-heart "giving," by which clarity and honesty become a method of healing. Being open with another who has hurt you also frees the other's honesty and clarity. When truth is revealed, respect and truth in the hearts of those involved—the givers and the receivers— grow in relationship, and in many cases they become closer to one another in love and respect.

Why Enough Is Not Good Enough

As practitioners or aspirants of generosity, we are restless and not interested in giving what is acceptable by normal standards of behaviour. We strive to give more. We go further. We surprise by our generosity. We change hearts by giving more than enough. The quantity bespeaks a commitment to break through the existing inertia as an investment in creativity, as the impetus for something truly generative. Giving enough is usually a safe, feel-good place. But there is an awareness, a different experience, when we choose to subsidize abundance. If we give just enough we are in effect minimizing our duties (which remain mostly "about me") and not engendering *hope* for others. If instead we go the extra mile (with open heart and with the dignity of others in mind), we become a vital cog in the ever-increasing circle of giving, receiving and circulating.

Once upon

~

A TROUBLED MARRIAGE

He was rarely home, and when he was he watched television. They slept in separate beds now. Money was tight, and sometimes the pressure was too much to bear. The children were now in their teens and leaving home.

She had to get away, get some perspective, take a course, do something to avoid the monotony. She went on a retreat about forgiveness. She couldn't sleep; she sat by the woodstove in the group room at night, looking out on the snow-covered fields and dead trees. She felt sorry for herself and her plight. Should she leave the marriage? She pondered the advice of the group leader, who had suggested she write a love letter to her husband. What could she say? And as she thought of him—who he had been to her, why they had married, the very source of his soul—she began to weep.

Did she love him now?

Words emerged between her sobs, and then pages and pages of them. She was astounded at how much she had to say about him—who he was to her. She had never told him any of this before. She hadn't thought you had to, once you were married. She worked on her letter, refining it, adding to it. As the weekend came to an end, she was excited about bringing forth the words that had been hidden for years in her heart, into her letter to him.

She rolled it up as a scroll, with a ribbon and a seal of wax, and handed it to him a few days after her return home. She needed to be prepared to do it at the right time.

He didn't say anything for a week, but she noticed his face had softened, his eyes were less absent. He had begun to smile and he noticed her again. When he reached for her hand across the table at supper he looked at her as he had on their first date. It was like beginning again.

NB: Our most pressing creativity in life is to be artful and constant in our "double-and" loving. This means opting to become filler-uppers for those we love. We must be aware of when generosity is becoming lost in busyness, when love is being buried in monotony. As in anything that aspires to be generative, we must concentrate on what matters. Those we love need to know of our love again and again and again.

～

BEING GENEROUS ANYWAY

Hold not a deed of little worth, thinking "This is little to me." The falling of drops of water will in time fill a water jar.

The Dhammapada

The charge from participating in circulating is "to be generous anyway." Being generous anyway—whatever happens—creates the surplus of love and receptivity that often heals the person who has hurt you, renews the environment in which the hurt was expressed and in the end provides peace in one's deepest self. We have found that usually the people most unlikely to be generous surprise us by responding to our generosity with their own desire to more fully participate in circulating by their own giving. No generous act goes unnoticed in another's consciousness. If you practise "double-and" thinking and extra-mile loving, then you illustrate how the art of right living works. We are all called to generous living; for some it is an easier art than for others. For some it requires healing to practise; those healed can then lead those who need healing.

We return again to the basic premise (introduced at the beginning of the book) that natural practitioners of generosity are at home in its ten virtues—*courage, discernment, humility, compassion, mercy, reliability, trust, hope, remembering* and *balance*. We become reliable practitioners of these virtues when ready to be:

- a willing problem solver (not evading or avoiding but embracing problems to find immediate solutions and act on them);
- a ready giver, a "yes" person, in the call and flow of circulating (spontaneously responding positively when needed);
- a need finder (being aware through a thinking heart of the needs of others, and sharing this received wisdom with them and others);
- an opportunity multiplier ("double-and" thinking and extra-mile loving);

- a truth teller (breaking through the barriers of murky assumptions, prejudices or behaviours to insist on what's fair);
- a community maker (leading by example, and giving priority to outcome, not ego);
- a filler-upper (giving not only what's needed but also what heals, restores and energizes);
- a fore-giver (providing what another needs before he or she knows it's needed).

We can refine our practice of the art of generosity by consistently checking our answers to the following questions.

- Have I given freely where needed?
- Have I listened to the opportunity within the need?
- Have I consciously and graciously received?
- Am I consistent in my expression to those I love and care for?
- Have I attended to the details required of me?
- Have I appreciated others?
- Have I openly shared the gifts of myself and my creativity in community?

- Do I need to learn more from others?
- Am I living in gratitude?
- Am I constantly changing for the better?
- Do I put love into action as growth in my heart, or am I inclined to wait and see?
- Have I risked healing what is broken in myself, in my family, among my friends, at work or in my community?
- Have I remembered that small everyday things done with great love make a difference in the world?
- Have I noticed and acknowledged the generosity of constantly generous people in my life?

These questions are intended not as a definitive prescription but to help as a grounding reflection on the everyday priorities in the art of right living. They can provide a daily examination of matters of the heart. They can also be signposts to redirect you when busyness takes over. They can point the way when you become confused by the churn of otherwise meaningless activities.

Generosity calls us to embody its gentle and powerful ways in our own attitude and actions. If you find that giving, receiving and circulating can be *your* way of life, then remember that the place to begin—and come round to again and again— is giving first (and not wondering what you will be receiving before you do), receiving what is given with acceptance and gratitude, and being aware that the circumstances for circulating will reveal themselves in due time.

EIGHT

A Spiritual Ecology

———

We end this exploration of generosity in practice by sharing its nature, not only as an art of physical and social life, but also as a spiritual path. Even if you have a particular spiritual practice already, or a religious affiliation, the practice of generosity can only complement that commitment. If you do not follow any particular prayer tradition, then recognizing the value of making generosity a spiritual practice may enhance, and add a necessary discipline to, what could otherwise be a more *ad hoc* attitude and approach to spirituality.

OUR INTERIOR SELVES

Those of us who are able to practise times of silence—whether through contemplation and reflection, or quiet prayer and meditation—are aware of the vast store of riches we have inside ourselves. Within each of us lies a treasure chest of everything we need to live in joy and peace, to enable our consciousness to grow and discern, to plumb our depths for wisdom, to meet and unite our souls with love divine. This is where we are meant to begin all our actions, from the desire and calling from *within*. It is as if we unfold into the outer world from our inner world, rooted in the fertile soil of silence and prayer so that we can grow towards the light of the Divine, swaying in the fair breezes and bending with the more forceful winds that accompany life's frequent storms.

As vital as our hearts, and at the very core of life, our souls carry the DNA of transcendence that makes possible our capacity for love, peace and joy. When our souls are undernourished, they need our urgent attention, our generosity, in order to be filled with the consciousness that recognizes, receives and passes on grace. Just as our hearts pump blood vital for our bodies, our souls require us to give ourselves time, receive contemplative renewal and circulate the wisdom that emerges from within, in order to nourish our interior life. We have found that our spiritual diet requires us to pray and meditate daily; each month gain knowledge from theological reading and study; and each year renew ourselves by making a retreat or pilgrimage. As we give attention to our souls, we begin to feel the comfort of grace renewed in us. We feel a relationship with God through receiving divine sustenance, as well as the enormous gifts of growing faith and unity. In turn we eventually are able to circulate and partake in the power of this grace—the extraordinary manifestation of opportunities given to us—to enable us to be grace-full: that is, trying to be courteous, kind, attentive, grateful, responsive and generous to the people and situations we encounter. When our souls are fed, everything shifts into the flow of grace, enabling giving, receiving and circulating to be as natural as the air we breathe. Instead of being a project or a plan, generosity overflows and becomes an art all by itself—effortless, sublime and infused with an eternal fragrance beyond our imaginings and hopes. This delicate balance of living generosity as a spiritual practice takes some dedication and resolve. Like all magnificence, it can't align aspiration with practice without a dutiful development of consciousness.

BECOMING CONSCIOUS

The Wonder of our consciousness which we
Neglect to explore in depth, although we see
That it and it alone provides the cast
That makes the universe so huge and vast,
That it and it alone supplies the base
For all the immensity of time and space,
That it and it alone allots the size,
The shape and form which we mark with our eyes,
Also the number, distance and the span
Of time we try to calculate and scan.

Gopi Krishna

Consciousness, from a spiritual perspective, means becoming aware of the numinosity in one's inner life. It is about perceiving how this inner reality lives in the outer world, how all is united and whole beyond the illusion of separation and ego. Being immersed in transcendence means also being responsive to what, in normal circumstances, seems to be impossible. It is awakening to seeing anew; it is having your true wits about you. Literally, to be conscious means being alert to the signs of our times, and to the larger positive (and frequently threatening) forces at play in our social and spiritual evolution. It is about comprehending these, seeing the archetypical and mythic architecture of a grander plan. It is about being sagacious, and shrewd, and it is, as the Buddhists call it, being "mindful," emptying our personal thoughts so as to be filled with the themes of the great mind. It is about being awake in the moment to the gifts of graces, recognizing the hand of Divine Providence in the connection between cause and effect. It is about finding a way of existing—living without your heart and your mind being only half awake, and without your ego as the head of your interior household.

Spiritual teachers speak of this "mindfulness" as realizing an underlying unity to reality. Any generous act or prayer, any generous thought or idea therefore impacts unity and has cosmic ramifications. For being rich in faith, Gemma Dalla Costa did not let the impoverishment and struggles of her life preclude giving and circulating. She prayed for others, on her knees and while doing her work. She prayed with quiet diligence and decades-long dedication, to petition for others graces she did not experience herself, to extend comfort she did not have, to be a constant friend despite her losses, and to hope in the power of the Spirit for people who had less reason to despair than she. Generosity is God's popular virtue, one of the ways by which we recognize, appreciate and venerate the Divine and conform our human life to that divine reality. When no one else notices, God does, for such is the flow of love. Many religions teach that God chalks up our giving in our own personal karmic accounts. Karma's premise is about accountability for actions, but it is also infinitely more subtle. Giving, receiving and circulating not only defines the output of our lives as a measure of their virtue but also prepares us for

the possibility of participating in the fullest experience of divine love.

Karma is, as the American writer and teacher
Georg Feuerstein describes it, "the moral force of
one's intentions, thoughts and behavior . . .
karma refers to fate as determined by the quality
of one's being in past lives and the present life.
The underlying idea is that even the moral
dimension of existence is causally determined."
Hinduism and Buddhism teach that karma is
linked with reincarnation—that we choose to
incarnate to purify our karmic debts from past
lives. Even if we do not believe in reincarnation,
most religions imply that our thoughts and our
actions carry a spiritual responsibility, that we
affect the environment by the way we think and
act. We believe we affect our souls by the way we
think and act. We are shown the very real results
of our thoughts and actions by the relationships,
challenges and extraordinary synchronicities that
unfold in our lives. As regards generosity, the
purity of intention and of the heart, and the practice of the virtues applied to our attitude and
actions (discussed at length in this book), all cul-
minate in either good or bad karma being put into

the world. One either contributes to life or takes away from it. We are either generous or mean. Whatever our decisions, when we are conscious of the greater infinite reality we can see how much we are invited to contribute. Just being alive bestows the responsibility to share.

THE GENERATIVE SPIRIT

Most religions teach generosity. Some do so more obviously and dogmatically than others. Many are formed on processes for action, such as the yogic path of karma yoga, which is one of unselfish active giving, a duty done without fear of punishment or hope of reward. In practice one learns to discard the rewards of one's actions, caring about consequence, not attribution, which leads to a state of abiding inner peace. In the yoga traditions one's life realizes its entirety or wholeness through devotion to a surrender involving mindful and detached generosity. The key again is not outcomes but interior transformation, a conversion from one mode of consciousness to another.

Without necessarily using the same words as yoga, Taoism teaches a similar framework of giving, receiving and circulating in what is perceived as the spiritual stages of human life. As you grow in consciousness through early adult life, you give devotion to The Way, life to children, love to your neighbour, duty to community. In middle age you practise receiving—receiving the grace and the flow of The Way; you transition from a primary "outflowing" to take in more of life's meaning and treasures, and "diligently heat the roots of consciousness and life." With the turmoil of identity and career largely resolved, with the obligations of creating family, character and reputation largely past, this withdrawing phase becomes a "kindling light to all close at hand . . . And there hidden, let thy true self always dwell."

The secret of learning to receive in middle age is to gradually and gracefully withdraw from the activities of incessant giving to the opportunities of receivement. Becoming less of the ego-driven self and more of the surrendered soul is about letting go of that which is unnecessary at this stage of life. For many of us, this simplicity of life is what we long for, and frequently find difficult to embrace.

With a dose of humility and honesty, we may be able to recognize that this turning away from distractions to simplicity, from exhaustive giving to the recovery of quietly receiving, is, in truth, a constant requirement of the maturing soul.

Ever-practical Eastern spiritual teachings on one's senior years involve circulating, which begins in many guises. One may become a source of wisdom in the quiet seclusion of the slower years, a sort of wisdom school personified for those of younger generations who wish to learn. Also, one may close down old modes of communicating in favour of ones of deeper significance in later life. Silence is valued—words are weighed with greater awareness and careful discernment, activities are curtailed or more focused, and times for contemplating the expansive landscape of consciousness are grasped enthusiastically. When advanced in Taoism, grandparents withdraw to be absorbed into the mists of time. By doing so, they make space for new life to flower and contribute to the start of a fresh cycle of giving, receiving and circulating, as they move on.

In Judaism, the life path is described in different terms and yet is premised on a similar threefold trajectory, which Rabbi and Professor Arthur Green calls the "Three Pillars." The first inexhaustible treasure of Judaism—its primary pillar—is the Torah. The study of the law can never be complete, either for the individual or for the community, as it expresses the living word of God, and provides glimpses into God's unfathomable transcendence based on relationship. For Jews, the Torah is received—God's law bequeathed on Sinai, confirming both Covenant and freedom, given to a people in community. The spiritual practice is to give one's life to its study, becoming an embodiment of what lives and circulates God's will.

The second pillar of worship involves daily prayer, Torah readings and community festivals, by which those who have received God's law give back veneration, devotion, repentance and charity. Giving is a form of prayer; prayer again is a communal offering. With the third pillar— compassion—Jews are charged with the moral obligation to share with those in need, especially the most vulnerable, whom the prophet Isaiah named as "the widow, the orphan, the naked, the homeless and the imprisoned" (1:17).

The Covenant is between realms, between heaven and Earth, and its stipulations are to live in a heavenly way, that is, with generosity, on Earth. Scholars who have studied the historical context of Covenant explain that this is in no way like our modern notion of contract. With Covenant, blessings and obligations are exchanged, not as reciprocity, but in superfluity, since this is necessary to enable freedom, dignity and community justice. In Covenant, we receive more than any one of us deserves, so as to give more as individuals, and circulate the excess that allows those in most desperate need to also realize their dignity as children of God.

For Muslims, the third requirement within the foundational Five Pillars of Islam identifies alms-giving as *zakāt*. This means to "purify or increase." Faith in one God as creator of all beings confers equality in dignity and obligation. Islam teaches that the giver who shares wealth with the poor and needy is assured of increased blessings in this world and rich rewards in the next life. It is the Muslim understanding of the workings of grace, the natural circulating of God's blessings that humans have received and are therefore responsible for sharing. Not only are the gifts, like grace, given to those in need, but the acts themselves are part of devotional prayer. The actions are prayerful and humble offerings to God, which God repays in God's measure. The gifts of God's mercy, compassion and justice involve balance on Earth to mirror and attain the completing balance in paradise. Fasting at the time of Ramadan is important because it brings the whole community into equality and alignment in a generous sacrifice, one people make to experience hunger in order to be in solidarity with the hungry, and to be in community in realizing the abundance of God's gracious gifts.

In the Christian Gospels, Jesus instructs his followers very clearly about giving, receiving and circulating. In Luke he states: "Give and it will be given to you" (6:38). In John he teaches: "Ask and you shall receive" (16:24). And in Luke again, he reminds followers that "The measure you give will be the measure you get back" (6:38). As we would expect from a Jewish rabbi, Jesus is not interested in a simple symmetry between giving and receiving, but rather in the emptying out of ego that surrenders one to God's will and circulates what enables life and freedom for others. At the heart of this generosity is forgiveness, which circulates the mercy and acceptance we receive from God, enabling our mercy and acceptance for those who may have "trespassed against us." The obligation of giving as a participation in circulating is particularly evident in Jesus' Sermon on the Mount: "Blessed are those who hunger and thirst for righteousness, for they will be filled," "Blessed are the merciful, for they will receive mercy," and "Blessed are the peacemakers for they will be called children of God" (Matthew 5:3). The teaching here, considered essential to Christian discipleship, is to give ourselves over to God's sense of generosity, which is radically different from our own. In one teaching that summarizes this effusive circulating, Jesus says that from "All those who have been given more, more will be expected" (Matthew 25:29).

MORE FROM BEING LESS

It is worth pondering what this "more" is. It certainly lives in the receiving part of generosity, that what we have received—even life itself—is evidence of the generosity of the creative God. And, as receiving is a harder spiritual state to be in—in the prayer of quiet—it is natural for us to be given time and energy away from being receptive in order to be able to give in circulation. And the more we receive, the more we naturally wish to circulate. A woman we know who was a practitioner of karma yoga all her life, a real giver, is finding it difficult, almost impossible, to be a receiver as she grows older and her body is not as strong in bearing the weight of giving as it once was. She admits that she is in crisis because she has viewed herself only as a giver, a one-way heartbeat for others. Yet she cannot struggle on, she has to listen, she has to let go into her God, and she says it is the hardest spiritual work she has ever done, moving from this interior attachment to what we define as our way, to where we are being led in God's way. And, as perfection itself unfolds, we almost see the wisdom of the Divine in discovering that in the quiet we recognize our vast abundance; in the stillness we offer our past activities; in the listening we hear more clearly the voice of the Divine's will for us.

We have noted that generosity is about changing, and the generosity of the Divine Spirit always forces us to change, pushes us gently, nudges us from the supposed safety of our status quo, to the risks of the unknown. Many of us feel that we have to do something in order to receive the reward of life. In the spiritual life the charge is to share who we are by being an example of the Spirit's generosity to each of us. It is vital to be generous *to* the Divine through spending time in developing our spiritual relationship by the practice of prayer, meditation, study and ritual.

A spiritual practice is about developing a higher awareness of one's soul, one's higher self, so that our hearts are purer and wiser when it comes to discernment, and are practised in the art of loving. A private practice of prayer and meditation allows us to develop, learn and grow; it helps us become more conscious of not only ourselves and others, but also our God, known to us by our own particular names. Through a spiritual practice, we begin to know the God deep within us. And from this time given to spiritual relationship, God will give back hundredfold. Giving ourselves in prayer means we receive what God wishes to give us; when we receive we circulate God's special graces through us, not in any personally informed way, but just by being prayerful and making the sacred central in our day. This way we become the messengers of a generous deity. We are able to recognize other messengers of the sacred, and then a community is formed to share, in the outer circle, this eternal and loving generosity of God.

In organized religions, shared rituals are a way of bringing together communities in common prayer, in order to make their community a sacrament, a holy whole. In Taoism the Tao is in circulation when it is allowed to freely move, when a practitioner is aware of its varied rhythms and abides with them. Invariably the best determinant is the awareness of the intervals between the movements. Observing Buddhism's moral obligations of not killing, stealing, committing adultery, lying, drinking alcohol or eating meat enables the practitioner's consciousness to be undistracted and grow into purity. The challenge is the interior practice of these obligations—no killing of truth, or stealing in one's mind, or experiencing the temptations and impurities of an unconscious life. As Buddhist teachings are based on compassion for all, including oneself, they are the basis of non-harming of all living creatures. The generosity is towards all of creation—all of nature and all life within it. As American theologian Rosemary Radford Ruether wrote in her book *Gaia & God*, "Human consciousness, then, should not be what utterly separates us from the rest of 'nature.' Rather, consciousness is where this dance of energy organizes itself in increasingly unified ways, until it reflects back on itself in self-awareness."

NO ONE IS AN ISLAND

"Our existence as embodied beings is purely momentary; what are a hundred years in eternity? But if we shatter the chains of egotism, and melt into the ocean of humanity, we share its dignity. To feel that we are something is to set up a barrier between God and ourselves; to cease feeling that we are something is to become one with God."

Mahatma Gandhi (Mohan-Mālā)

Archbishop of Canterbury Rowan Williams echoed Gandhi's quote in a paper he delivered in April 2005 at Oxford University: "Self-forgetting brings joy, common, shared joy." We cannot forget ourselves unless we remember God. We forget ourselves only when we see how small we are in relation to the larger plan unfolding around us. We participate in and contribute to the generosity of the Divine's creation only by forgetting the relatively trivial problems of self and embracing the mega problems we are faced with, such as our fatigued Earth, which tirelessly and generously provides for us despite our unconscious abuse, and is fast becoming exhausted. This is not a responsibility for others; the Earth is generous to each one of us and we each, in turn, need to be generous with it. And, according to the laws of karma, we must ask ourselves what we are consciously doing to contribute to the goodness we have been given.

Without a disciplined and committed spiritual practice, we can remain impervious to the Divine's generous presence. With silence and prayer we can effect the change within our own self to effect change around us; with prayer we can heal, restore, renew and contribute. One woman we know, who has been always generous with us, committed to praying a rosary a day—a half-hour of repetitive prayer—in support of and solidarity with an artist struggling to bring an artwork to completion. An offer of intention and love, her prayers embraced and surrounded her friend while simulating the difficult effort of birthing creativity. The grace of her gift can be seen as a masterpiece that linked, laboured and aligned with the masterpiece finally completed by her friend. Without prayer and meditation, we are open to all the hazards of *un*consciousness, even though we hold to our best intentions. Intentions are to be mindful, therefore meditative; intentions are projects for our hearts, requiring religious imagination and spiritual practice to purify and strengthen our souls, and elevate awareness of our debts, contributions and spiritual growth and changes.

While almost all the traditional religions teach the necessity of kindness, fairness and compassion, one task for our time and spiritual diversity is to aggressively practise generosity towards each other regardless of belief.

- We need to share our human wisdom, spiritual insights and soul experiences, and allow others to share theirs with us.
- We need to be recipients of respect from others towards our private beliefs and prayers, as we need to be respectful of others, whatever their faith or belief.
- We need to circulate by being mindful—aware, respectful and sensitive—of others in public spaces and communal places we use in our everyday lives.
- We need to contribute to the peace we all desire. This may seem an insignificant thing, like being aware that our cellphone conversation is not only unimportant to others, but disturbs their moments of reflection or enjoyment, or by being conscious of our impact on the solitude of others—of how we contribute to noise pollution by blowing our car horns, shouting on streets, slamming doors, playing loud music, drilling and hammering while renovating our houses, without notice or concern for the needs of our neighbours.

We are not islands. We are all, each one of us, part of the human "mainland"—an integrated, interconnected, sometimes volatile, often beautiful, exasperating and exhilarating community.

- We need, therefore, to be welcoming to those we don't know, to be courteous to strangers whether on the street or when speaking with them on the telephone.
- We need to use our reflective times to circulate by praying for those who can't stop, are sick or are in need, and we need to be able to receive by asking for prayers from others when we too are running short of time, perspective or peace.
- We need to notice and absorb the exquisiteness of creation, or how poor are we? And we need to relish the unconditional love of the Earth, providing sustenance.
- We need to know that we are not really safe or secure in anything that does not last—that only the infinite order of all things and the unconditional love of the Divine endure.
- We need to remember that our prayer time and spiritual practices are acts of generosity

to the Divine, that offer service to others and are ultimately imperative for ourselves.

- We need to remember that generosity is not ours, but is the Divine's grace that binds our souls in an eternal embrace of giving, receiving and circulating.

In the end we all pass from this Earth. The significance of our lives will then rest in what we have creatively and lovingly contributed to others, through our attitude, our thoughts, our prayers, words, deeds, work and art.

THE STREAM OF LIFE

*The same stream of life that runs through my veins
night and day runs through the world and dances in
rhythmic measures.*

*It is the same life that shoots in joy through the dust
of the earth in numberless blades of grass and
breaks into tumultuous waves of leaves and flowers.*

*It is the same life that is rocked in the ocean-cradle
of birth and of death, in ebb and in flow.*

*I feel my limbs made glorious by the touch of this
world of life. And my pride is from the life-throb of
ages dancing in my blood this moment.*

Rabindranath Tagore.

ACKNOWLEDGMENTS

⁓

We are grateful for the risks, courage, creativity and kindnesses of so many who have provided us with living examples of generosity in action. These include not only friends and family but heroes for peace and justice whose stories continually inspire us.

We especially appreciate Diane Martin for receiving our work so lovingly and enthusiastically, for giving suggestions to make it better and involving so many in its circulation. We are thankful too for Linda McKnight's comforting and constant friendship (and early editorial notes), and for Louise Dennys' generous mind, heart and support.

For all those who have touched this book in a special way, who have contributed their personal gifts to its coming together in editing and design through those involved in its printing, marketing and distribution, we offer our sincere gratitude.

Neither of us could have written this book alone, so each of us is thankful for the other. And within our collaboration we principally honour the intercession of the One whose spirit lives within us and this work.

Lucinda Vardey & John Dalla Costa

BIBLIOGRAPHICAL REFERENCES

INVITATION

"O May I Join the Choir Invisible," by George Eliot, quoted in part from *The Legend of Jubal and Other Poems* (Toronto: Adam, Stevenson, 1874, Fisher Rare Book Library).

Mother Teresa: A Simple Path, compiled by Lucinda Vardey (New York: Ballantine Books, 1995).

"Wealth without Work," from *The Seven Blunders*, by M.K. Gandhi (M. K. Gandhi Institute for Non-Violence *www.gandhiinstitute.org*, 1947).

CHAPTER 1: PREPARING FOR POSSIBILITIES

The City of God, by St. Augustine, translated by Henry Bettenson (London: Penguin Books Ltd., 1972).

"A Greeting to the Virtues," from *The Writings of St. Francis of Assisi*, edited by Halcyon Backhouse (London: Headline Book Publishing PLC, 1994).

The Power of Compassion: A Collection of Lectures by His Holiness the XIV Dalai Lama, translated by Geshe Thupten Jinpa (London: Thorsons, 1995).

Tao Te Ching, by Lao Tzu, translated by D. C. Lau (London: Penguin Books Ltd., 1963).

Nicomachean Ethics, by Aristotle, edited by Roger Crisp (Cambridge, England: Cambridge University Press, 2000).

Trust: The Social Virtues and the Creation of Prosperity, by Francis Fukuyama (London: Hamish Hamilton Ltd., 1995).

The Ethics of Memory, by Avishai Margalit (Cambridge, MA: USA: Harvard University Press, 2002).

Holy Bible: New Revised Standard Version (Nashville, TN: Catholic Bible Press, 1991).

Wellsprings: A Book of Spiritual Exercises, by Anthony de Mello (New York: Doubleday & Co., 1986).

Revelations of Divine Love, by Julian of Norwich, translated by Elizabeth Spearing (London: Penguin Books Ltd., 1991).

CHAPTER 2: WIDENING THE VIEW

Wellsprings: A Book of Spiritual Exercises, by Anthony de Mello (New York: Doubleday & Co., 1986).

Reclaiming Dietrich Bonhoeffer: The Promise of His Theology, by Charles Marsh (New York: Oxford University Press, 1994).

Some Reflections on Philanthropy, by James M. Purcell (Santa Clara, CA: Santa Clara University *www.scu.edu/ignatian center/bannan/publications*, 2005).

Good to Great, by James Collins (New York: HarperCollins
    Publishers Inc., 2001).

CHAPTER 3: A SYMPHONY OF THREE
Pierre Teilhard de Chardin: Writings selected by Ursula King
    (Maryknoll, NY, Orbis Books, 1993).
Genevieve Vaughan's Selected Writings ("The Gift Economy,"
    www.gift-economy.com).
The Harmony Project (*www.theharmonyproject.org*).
"Overcoming the Divided Life," by Michael J. Naughton,
    in *Business As Calling: Interdisciplinary Essays on the
    Meaning of Business from the Catholic Social Tradition*,
    edited by Michael J. Naughton and Stephanie Rumpza
    (E-book: St. Paul, MN: Center for Catholic Studies,
    University of St. Thomas, 2005).
*The Alphabet versus the Goddess: The Conflict between Word
    and Image*, by Leonard Shlain (New York: Arkana,
    The Penguin Group, 1999).
"Lord, make me an instrument of your peace." attributed to
    St. Francis of Assisi (no known source).

CHAPTER 4: GIVING
"The extra-mile" Matthew 5:41, Holy Bible.
Mother Teresa: A Simple Path, compiled by Lucinda Vardey
    (New York: Ballantine Books, 1995).
*The Need for Roots: Prelude to a Declaration of Duties towards
    Mankind*, by Simone Weil, translated by A. F. Wills
    (London: Routledge, 1995).

CHAPTER 5: RECEIVING

Anonymous prayer by seventeenth-century nun from *The Flowering of the Soul: A Book of Prayers by Women,* edited by Lucinda Vardey (Toronto: Alfred A. Knopf, 1999).

"Eucharistic Prayer for the Feast of Corpus Christi," by St. Augustine (*www.scs.sk.ca*, 2005).

Letter to Robert Hooke, February 5, 1675, by Isaac Newton. (www.quotationspage.com/quotes/Isaac_Newton/).

Mother Teresa: A Simple Path, compiled by Lucinda Vardey (New York: Ballantine Books, 1995).

"The Primacy of Receivement," by John Haughey SJ, in *Business As Calling: Interdisciplinary Essays on the Meaning of Business from The Catholic Social Tradition,* edited by Michael J. Naughton and Stephanie Rumpza (E-book: St. Paul, MN: Center for Catholic Studies, University of St. Thomas, 2005).

CHAPTER 6: CIRCULATING

The Righteous: The Unsung Heroes of the Holocaust, by Martin Gilbert (Toronto: Key Porter Books Limited, 2003).

The Phenomenon of Man, by Pierre Teilhard de Chardin, translated by Bernard Wall (New York: Perennial, HarperCollins Publishers Inc., 2002).

The Foundation: A Great American Secret—How Private Wealth Is Changing the World, by Joel L. Fleishman (New York: PublicAffairs, Perseus Books Group, 2006).

"Japanese billionaire hands over multimillion-dollar homes to low-income families." News syndicate item published March 22, 2007 (Canadian Press).

CHAPTER 7: THE ART OF THE HEART

Edith Stein: Scholar, Feminist, Saint, by Freda Mary Oben,
   PhD (New York: Alba House, 1988).

*An Interrupted Life: The Diaries, 1941–1943, and Letters from
   Westerbork,* by Etty Hillesum, translated by Arnold J.
   Pomerans (New York: Henry Holt and Company, 1996).

"Lord, make me an instrument of your peace." attributed to
   St. Francis of Assisi (no known source).

Journey of the Mind to God, by St. Bonaventure, translated
   by P. Boelmer (Indianapolis: Hackette Publishing
   Company Ltd, 1993).

The Dhammapada: The Path of Perfection, translated from
   the Pali by Juan Mascaró (London: Penguin Books
   Ltd., 1973).

CHAPTER 8: A SPIRITUAL ECOLOGY

The Riddle of Consciousness, "What is Cosmic Consciousness?"
   by Gopi Krishna (New York: The Central Institute
   for Kundalini Research and The Kundalini Research
   Foundation, Ltd., 1976).

The Encyclopedic Dictionary of Yoga, by Georg Feuerstein
   (New York: Paragon House, 1990).

The Secret of the Golden Flower: A Chinese Book of Life, by
   Richard Wilhelm (London, Penguin Books Ltd 1984).

*Seek My Face, Speak My Name: A Contemporary Jewish
   Theology,* by Rabbi Arthur Green (Northvale, NJ:
   Jason Aronson Inc., 1994).

World Religions: Western Traditions, edited by Willard G.
   Oxtoby (Toronto: Oxford University Press, 1996).

Gaia & God: An Ecofeminist Theology of Earth Healing, by Rosemary Radford Ruether (San Francisco: HarperSanFrancisco, HarperCollins Publishers, 1994).

Mohan-Mālā (A Gandhian Rosary), compiled by R. K. Prabhu (Ahmedabad: Navajivan Publishing House, 1949).

Creation, Creativity and Creatureliness: the Wisdom of Finite Existence, lecture by Rowan Williams, Archbishop of Canterbury (Oxford: St. Theosevia Centre for Christian Spirituality, 2005).

"The Stream of Life," from *The Heart of God: Prayers of Rabindranath Tagore*, selected by Herbert F. Vetter (Boston, MA: Charles E. Tuttle Co., Inc., 1997). Used by permission of Tuttle Publishing, a member of the Periplus Publishing Group.

ABOUT THE AUTHORS

LUCINDA VARDEY is a teacher of spiritual life and author of many books on contemporary spirituality, including *God in All Worlds: An Anthology of Contemporary Spiritual Writing; The Flowering of the Soul: A Book of Prayers by Women;* the *New York Times* bestseller on Mother Teresa, *A Simple Path; Traveling with the Saints in Italy: Contemporary Pilgrimages on Ancient Paths* and a novel, *Blessed.* She is married to John Dalla Costa and lives in Tuscany and Toronto. *www.dallaluce.com*

JOHN DALLA COSTA is the founder of the Centre for Ethical Orientation, an international consultancy working on ethics, trust and governance. He has an advanced management degree (OPM) from Harvard Business School, and a master's degree in Divinity (summa cum laude) from Regis College, University of Toronto. His books include *Meditations on Business, Working Wisdom, The Ethical Imperative* and *Magnificence at Work: Living Faith in Business. www.ceo-ethics.com*

A NOTE ABOUT THE TYPE

Pierre Simon Fournier *le jeune*, who designed the type used in
this book, was both an originator and a collector of types. His
services to the art of print communication were his design of
individual characters, his creation of ornaments and initials and
his standardization of type sizes. Fournier types are old style in
character and sharply cut. In 1764 and 1766 he published his
Manuel typographique, a treatise on the history of French types
and printing, on typefounding in all its details and on what many
consider his most important contribution to the printed word—
the measurement of type by the point system.

BOOK DESIGN BY CS RICHARDSON